MY CONFERENCE CAN BEAT YOUR CONFERENCE

WHY THE SEC *STILL* RULES COLLEGE FOOTBALL

PAUL FINEBAUM

AND GENE WOJCIECHOWSKI

HARPER

www.harpercollins.com

HarperCollins books may be purchased for educational, business, or sales promotional use. For information, please e-mail the Special Markets Department at SPsales@harpercollins.com.

FIRST EDITION

Designed by Renato Stanisic

Library of Congress Cataloging-in-Publication Data

Finebaum, Paul.
My conference can beat your conference : why the SEC still rules college football / Paul Finebaum.
        pages   cm
ISBN 978-0-06-229741-9
ISBN 978-0-06-236524-8 (Signed Edition)
1. Southeastern Conference—History. 2. Football—Southern States—History. I. Wojciechowski, Gene. II. Title.
GV958.5.S59F56   2014
796.332'630975—dc3   2014014199

14 15 16 17 18   OV/RRD   10 9 8 7 6 5 4 3 2

To college football fans everywhere—your passion helps
to make it the nation's greatest sport.

Contents

CONTENTS

I've known people from up north. They admire the SEC, but it's more hating and jealousy than anything else. If you admire something and you ain't got something, you just hate. If you can get the truth out of 'em, they admire the passion that people in the South have for football.

—DARRIEL FROM COLUMBUS, GEORGIA

We're No. 1! (Even When We're Not)

Friday, February 14, 2014
Charlotte, North Carolina

THE OFF-SEASON SKINNY: Just chillin' . . . Listening to Drake . . . Wondering if my pal Condi Rice will have the guts to vote for three SEC teams to the first-ever football final four.

One day it will happen. North Korea's Kim Jong-un will get wasted at a Sigma Chi party and give the missile launch codes to frat brother Dennis Rodman. Snooki will be elected the forty-fifth president of the United States. Maybe convergent plate tectonics will turn the Earth molten and do us in.

Whatever happens, I can guarantee you three things will survive the near-annihilation of the human race: the Kardashians . . . airline snack packs (pinto bean–flavored flax chips!) . . . and the Southeastern Conference.

The SEC is indestructible. The SEC is virtually unbeatable (I said, "virtually"—so don't get your shorts in a bunch, Florida State). It gargles with hydrochloric acid. It can bench-press the Big Ten Conference with Vanderbilt tied behind its back. If there were a scouting combine for conferences, the SEC would be the workout freak everyone raves about *and* the no-brainer No. 1 pick in the draft.

I'm not saying this because I'm bitter about FSU beating SEC champ Auburn in the sixteenth and, thankfully, final BCS Championship Game. I'm not saying this because I'm the Mouth of the South, or because I was born in the South, raised in the South, schooled in the South, make my living in the South, got married in the South and will eventually croak in the South. I'm saying it because it's true. You know it. I know it. Kim Jong-un and Florida State—they know it, too.

Red-blooded, pigskin-loving Americans everywhere recognize real college football when they see it. And real college football, the kind that puts hair on your chest, the kind that year after year makes those supposed big, bad teams in the Big Ten Conference, the Pac-12 Conference, the Big 12 Conference, the Atlantic Coast Conference, the Notre Dame Conference—and all the rest of them—reach for their pacifiers in fear, is played at the highest level in one place and one place only: the SEC.

If God made the world in seven days, He spent the eighth day in his two-car garage, sipping on a cold one, listening to Merle Haggard and dreaming up the SEC. And here's what He came up with: Fourteen (and counting) programs nestled in the proudest region on the planet. Winners of seven out of the last eight, and nine out of the sixteen BCS Championships. The last eight national championship games have featured at least one SEC team, sometimes two. The closest thing to a living, breathing football dynasty: the University of Alabama, led by its football generalissimo, Nick Saban. And the other team in that state, Auburn, led by play-calling savant Gus Malzahn, isn't so bad either.

The SEC is college football's version of Rome, the center of the football universe. Long may it rule.

The SEC has everything that all the other conferences want when they grow up: the best players, the most decadent football stadiums, the plushest and most over-the-top football facilities (with the possible exception of the University of Phil Knight, in Eugene, Oregon), the most obscene operating budgets, the highest-paid coaching staffs, the largest number of NFL draftees, the most meaningful traditions, the most twisted and hyperintense rivalries, the most devout and devious fans, the largest attendance figures, the best recruits (seven of the top ten–rated ESPN recruiting classes in 2014 belong to SEC teams; an SEC program has finished atop the ESPN recruiting rankings five of the last six years), the most obnoxious media days, the kind of personal scandals that give TMZ a reason to live, the highest TV ratings, some of the biggest merchandise revenue numbers and school-related vanity license plate sales, the most lucrative TV contracts, the most fun NCAA investigations, the most magnetic stars (before he left early for the NFL, Johnny Manziel was Elvis with shoulder pads), the most passionate anti–Urban Meyer faction, the most obnoxiously large marching bands and, of course . . . the most national title parades. Only the Magic Kingdom and Macy's have had more parades than the SEC.

The last thing the SEC and its rabid followers should ever do is apologize for their excesses. If anything, they should revel in them, celebrate them as if every day were Fat Tuesday. If the SEC were a car company, it would sell a tricked-out commemorative Bama-edition sport utility vehicle with every conceivable option: houndstooth upholstery, a center console/warming bin for Tuscaloosa's world-famous Dreamland ribs and, above all, a satellite radio system preset to me and my *Paul Finebaum Show.*

I never played a down of football. I'm built like a paper clip. I weigh a buck and change and wouldn't know a skinny post from the postmaster general. But I know what greatness looks like. It looks like the SEC.

The SEC is football's megachurch. It doesn't matter if you're in the first pew or the last, you're still part of the congregation. From College Station to Gainesville, we worship together. So give me an "Amen!" to that.

Find me a conference with a better commissioner, better players, better head coaches, better staffs, better game day atmosphere, better media coverage, better-looking coeds . . . better anything. While you're attempting to do that, I'll just go ahead and watch all eight Harry Potter movies. When I'm done, I'll go count all the empty Southern Comfort bottles after a game at LSU's Death Valley. And when I'm done with that, you *still* won't be able to find another league that can match the SEC pedigree for pedigree.

The Big Ten can't match it. The Big Ten can't win a Buffalo Wild Wings Bowl, much less a national championship. It had exactly one national title during the BCS Era, and it took a late, you've-got-to-be-kidding-me! pass interference penalty against Miami in overtime to help give Ohio State the much-debated victory. The coach of that Ohio State team, Jim Tressel, was such an upstanding guy that he was eventually fired for a rules cover-up and handed a five-year show-cause penalty by the NCAA.

For all the Big Ten's insufferable yammering about tradition, and The Shoe, and The Big House, and its alumni base, the conference has as many national championships in the last forty-five years (four) as the SEC has won in the last five. And, Big Ten fanatics, don't even think of trying to count Nebraska's national titles. The Cornhuskers won those when they were still members of the Big Eight or Big 12.

The ACC can't match it. First of all, the ACC keeps adopting new teams like they're puppies at the Humane Society. Six of its fourteen full-time football members have joined the conference since 2004, including three since 2013—four if you count Notre Dame, the purebred with delusions of grandeur.

The ACC is feeling pretty good about itself these days. It beat the big, bad SEC in the BCS Championship. That's great. Congratulations. Now win six more in a row and you can sit at the big-boy table with the SEC. And I'll stop talking.

Do you know how many ACC teams not named Florida State have won national championships since 1991? Zero. Do you know how many even played in one? That's right, zero.

If not for Florida State, ACC football would be the Mid-American

Conference on Red Bull. How do I say this delicately? When FSU joined the ACC in time for the 1992 season, the league, well, sucked. It was so dreadfully mediocre that FSU might well have been Troy Aikman's Dallas Cowboys. The Seminoles won the conference title the next nine years in a row. In twelve years, they lost six conference games—six! That says something about the quality of FSU football, but it says more about the miserable ACC.

So FSU won national championships in 1993, 1999 and now 2013. They almost won one in 1998 too, but the Seminoles got beat by an SEC team—Tennessee—in the first BCS National Championship.

The ACC has gotten better, I'll give it that. But Clemson still can't win a big game that counts for something, and it definitely can't beat the SEC's South Carolina. Steve Spurrier's Gamecocks have won five in a row against the in-state rivals—not that the Head Ball Coach is counting. Oh, wait, he is. The HBC counts everything and then lets Dabo Swinney know about it every chance he gets.

Duke was fun to watch in 2013, especially in its loss to the SEC's Texas A&M in the Chick-fil-A Bowl. Georgia Tech had its moments in the Music City Bowl loss to the SEC's Ole Miss.

I propose that FSU's rings from last season ought to read, "2013 SEC CHAMPIONS." After all, Noles coach Jimbo Fisher, a longtime former SEC assistant at Auburn, and later a Saban assistant at LSU, patterned his program after SEC powerhouses. Eight of Fisher's nine assistants from his 2013 championship team, as well as his strength and conditioning coach, his director of player personnel, his director of football operations and one of his three graduate assistants, have connections with SEC programs. His offense and defense use an SEC-style template. He even structured his BCS Championship Game preparations on what Saban did at Alabama.

Coincidence? Nuh, uh.

His Heisman Trophy–winning quarterback, Jameis Winston, was born and raised just forty-five minutes from Tuscaloosa. Winston is the only high school player Saban ever watched in person on a Friday night during a Bama regular season.

Fisher is no dummy. He understood that to beat an SEC team, he had to build an SEC team. And Florida State is an SEC team, which is really the highest compliment you can pay a football program. FSU might be an official member of the softish ACC, but its football program has SEC chromosomes.

The Big 12 can't match it. But at least the Big 12 makes the effort.

Let me restate not for the last time that the SEC won nine of the sixteen BCS Championships. Of the remaining seven titles in that period, the Big 12 won two (Oklahoma once, Texas once). Unlike the ACC, three different Big 12 teams reached the BCS title game (OU, Texas and Nebraska). Of course, those three different Big 12 teams went 0-3 vs. the SEC in those three different championship games, but that's just the HBC counting, right?

OU coach Bob Stoops popped off earlier in 2013, saying that the idea of SEC dominance was "propaganda." Big Game Bob said this only a few months after the SEC's Texas A&M humiliated his Sooners in the Cotton Bowl.

Stoops is a great coach. You don't win a national title and surpass Barry Switzer's victory total at OU by accident. But was it "propaganda" when Stoops lost the BCS National Championships to LSU in 2003 and to Florida in 2008?

And while we're on the subject of misinformation, maybe it's time to remind Stoops that the SEC has fourteen teams and the toughest conference championship this side of the NFL. The Big 12 has ten teams and no conference championship game.

Yes, Stoops's Sooners beat a semi-interested Bama team in last season's Sugar Bowl. That's nice, especially since OU hadn't played in a BCS bowl since the 2010 season (the Sooners beat an unranked Connecticut team in the Fiesta). Before that, Stoops had lost the 2008 BCS Championship to

Florida, the 2007 Fiesta to West Virginia, the 2006 Fiesta to Boise State and the 2004 BCS Championship to USC (by 36 points).

By the way, do you think Stoops was saying SEC dominance was propaganda when he was Florida's defensive coordinator and the Gators were winning the 1996 national championship against the ACC's death star, Florida State, as well as the next two bowl games UF played during his three-year stay there?

Florida coach Will Muschamp, who came to Gainesville after serving as Texas's defensive coordinator, nailed it when asked about Stoops's propaganda comments: "I'd say the same thing if I were in the Big 12. I said it for three years."

The Pac-12 can't match it. For all the talk about USC and Oregon, the two programs combined for exactly one BCS Championship. No other team in the conference has ever reached a title game. And the remaining conferences combined can't match it. The American Athletic? Conference USA? The MAC? The Mountain West? The Sun Belt?

Lovely kids. Competitive players. But compared with the SEC, their conferences are like the kids who have peanut allergies.

And the aforementioned Notre Dame can't match it.

The Irish are stubborn football independents, except for the part where they'll play four ACC games in 2014, six in 2015 and then five each year after that. In short, Notre Dame likes the ACC just enough NOT to be a football member.

Notre Dame always talks about how it wants to be the best. Well, then, how about scheduling the best? How about ditching the service academies and the ACC and try the SEC on a regular basis? Wouldn't it be fun to see how Notre Dame would do in the SEC West? You saw what Bama did to the Irish in the BCS Championship in 2012. Just think if ND has to play LSU, Bama, Arkansas, Ole Miss, A&M and Mississippi State, and make the occasional road trip to Gainesville, Athens, Knoxville and the two Columbias.

Trust me, Domers, Notre Dame football had the life span of Rudy's cultural relevance, which may have finally ended.

At the top of the SEC food chain is Alabama and the state's favorite control freak: Saban. All Saban has done is win three of the last five BCS National Championships and four of the last eleven (three at Bama, one at LSU). When the playoff system kicks in at the end of the 2014 season, Saban will figure out a way to win one of those too. Give him enough time and he'd figure out a way to win *American Idol*, the Iditarod and the North Dakota gubernatorial race.

Saban could coach a lingerie football team to the Big Ten Championship Game. He could coach an intramural team to the national semis. Yes, he can be secretive, manipulative, socially insufferable, dictatorial and imperial. And your point is . . . ?

In the SEC, the spring games are bigger than other non-SEC programs' regular-season games. Auburn drew 83,401 fans for its 2013 spring game. That's more fans than were at Notre Dame Stadium for last season's top-25 matchup between Oklahoma and the Fighting Irish. That's more fans than attended any Week One NFL game in 2013, with the exception of the New York Giants at the Dallas Cowboys.

Bama drew 78,315 fans for its spring games. Bama could draw 50,000 fans just for pregame calisthenics. Seven of the top ten spring-game attendance figures came from SEC programs.

I'll give Big Ten commish Jim Delany his due. He created the Big Ten Network out of thin air and it's become an ATM for that conference. He expanded his league into Pennsylvania, Maryland, New Jersey and Nebraska. He got his athletic directors and coaches to quit scheduling games against the Charleston Southerns/Jiffy Lubes of the world. He went to a nine-game conference schedule. He negotiated some killer TV deals, with more to come.

But I'll still take SEC commissioner Mike Slive over Delany and anybody else you want to nominate. I'll take Slive over NFL commissioner Roger Goodell. Or MLB's Uncle Bud. Or any of our U.S. cabinet members.

Ever been to the Sistine Chapel? Me neither. But I've seen plenty of photos of Michelangelo's fresco masterpiece. And if you look hard enough, I swear God's fingertip is touching the outstretched hand of Slive, not Adam. And in the background, amid the angels wearing sundresses and cowboy boots and ringing Mississippi State cowbells, you can see Eve shouting, "Roll Tide."

Let's be honest: the South is basically a four-sport town. We've got college football season, college football recruiting season, spring football season and NASCAR. Five of the eleven states in the SEC (Mississippi, Alabama, South Carolina, Arkansas and Kentucky) have exactly zero pro franchises (not counting the 2011–12 Kentucky Wildcat basketball team). There isn't really much else to do than to talk about college football. That's who we are, that's who we want to be and that's who we'll always be. You got a problem with that?

Admit it, Eastern elitists: you look down at us. You mock our twangs, our politics, our evangelicals, our mullets and our Honey Boo Boo–ness. You think we wrestle gators on weekends, buy our teeth at Wal-Mart and dream of one day owning a double-wide down by the river. You think our politicians are corrupt (and some of them are, just like yours in the North) and that our civil rights record is still stuck in the record grooves of the 1950s. You regionally profile us.

We have some insecurities in the South, I'll admit that. We have scar tissue and scab marks from our inglorious past. Yeah, we've got some work to do when it comes to social issues. What, you don't?

Still, it's as simple as this: when it comes to college football, the South has no equal because the SEC has no equal. We have so many trophies, banners and national titles that we rent storage space at the National Archives. Our championship teams have spent more time in the White House than the Secret Service. We've presented so many No. 1 jerseys to POTUS, he could open his own Dick's Sporting Goods.

Anytime you want to send down your best twenty-two against the SEC's best twenty-two, I'll be glad to bet my house against yours. In fact, just to make it a tiny bit more fair, forget about the SEC's best twenty-two—I'll take the best of the SEC West or the best of the SEC East against anything you've got. And I'll still spot you a touchdown. OK, two. Same deal goes for anybody who thinks the best ball is played on the West Coast, or in the Midwest or Southwest. I'd take the best twenty-two of the SEC against the Cleveland Browns tomorrow.

People outside the SEC look down on the South's obsession with college football. I look up to it. The SEC is college football's industrial giant. It makes us Southerners proud again. It helps define us. It makes us a family.

College football is our great equalizer. You've got Harvard, Wall Street and Independence Hall. We've got the Iron Bowl, Main Street and Kyle Field.

In 1984, as Alabama was in the midst of its first losing season in twenty-seven years, I was asked to give a speech in Gadsden, Alabama, which is about an hour outside Birmingham. I had been carving up second-year Alabama coach Ray Perkins in my newspaper columns and on the radio. I was merciless to the man who had had the misfortune of succeeding the great Bear Bryant. I had called Perkins and his players "chumps" and said the program was populated by a bunch of losers.

My speech was no different. I deconstructed the program like it was a cheap toy, and afterward this guy came up to me ten kinds of angry. You could have toasted marshmallows over his forehead.

"You have NO idea what you're talking about," he said, disgusted.

"Oh, yeah?" I said. "Why don't you explain it to me then."

I'm clever that way.

The man said he was a factory worker at the local Goodyear plant, and a Vietnam veteran whose tour of duty during the war had taken him to the demilitarized zone on the 17th parallel near the Ben Hai River. The vet told me he had often pulled night sentry duty and that the numbing monotony of the war was eclipsed only by the horror of what he had seen and heard during his time there. The jungle warfare. The death. The loneliness. The senselessness of it all.

He said his family would send him audiotapes of Alabama football games. They would arrive weeks after the games had actually been played, but it didn't matter to the soldier. He said those tapes were the only thing that made him want to live. He would listen to those Bama games and dream of coming back home, of watching Crimson Tide football again.

You can scoff at it if you'd like. My New York publisher probably does. The cynic in me wanted to. But you had to see his face, had to hear his voice, as he told the story. I have no doubt that Alabama football is what got him from one hellish Vietnam day to the next, and I learned what college football—in this case, Bama football—could mean to someone.

It took me a while, but I've become fluent in the language of the SEC. I look at a map of the U.S. and I see Birmingham—home of the SEC headquarters—as the nation's football capital. If there was a national anthem for the SEC, I could belt it out like Beyoncé. Without lip-synching.

You think a "mixed marriage" describes a couple's skin color? Nah—it's what you call an Auburn alum marrying a Bama alum. You assume the legend of Bear Bryant is manufactured folklore? Histrionics? Then you don't know just how much the Bear helped cauterize the bleeding of the South's shameful civil rights history. You don't buy into the growing legacy of Saban? Well, to quote one our greatest living actors, Mr. T: "Shut up, fool!"

The SEC isn't going anywhere, except to more trophy presentations and to the bank. It has a multibillion-dollar SEC Network deal with ESPN that runs through 2034. It has a multibillion-dollar broadcast deal with ESPN and a near-billion-dollar deal with CBS. It has its affiliations with assorted bowl games and will cash additional checks if one (or more) of its teams reaches the four-team national championship playoff.

According to the *Wall Street Journal*, there is a waiting list of 29,000 for Alabama season tickets. Texas A&M has a waiting list of 20,000. LSU and even Mississippi State have waiting lists.

SEC fatigue? How about SEC envy?

Hall of Fame sportswriter Rick Reilly wrote an entire column about it for ESPN.com. He rooted openly for Florida State to beat Auburn for no other reason than he was tired of watching SEC teams raising the BCS crystal football in triumph. In fact, he admitted that the column itself lacked reason. "It's leaking emotion from the bilge," he wrote. "It's journalistically wrong. I know. I just don't care."

Fair enough, Rick. FSU won, so now you don't have to dress backwards and take up the flugelhorn—as you promised to do if Auburn extended the SEC win streak to eight. But Reilly and the other critics have it all wrong. Why not root *for* greatness? By every imaginable and measurable standard, the SEC's championship run is one of the great streaks—if not THE greatest streak—in college football history. What makes it so fantastically impressive is how difficult it is to win the SEC. Sorry, Stoopsy, but Auburn had to beat two top-five teams (No. 1 Alabama in the Iron Bowl, followed by No. 5 Missouri in the SEC Championship) just to reach the BCS title game. Florida State didn't play a ranked team in its last four games of the regular season and faced No. 20 Duke in the ACC Championship.

FSU beat Auburn fair and square. But the second-best SEC team in 2012 was better than the No. 1–ranked Notre Dame team that got waxed and buffed by Alabama in the BCS Championship.

It was open season on the SEC in 2013—all because it was too successful. There were parts of eleven states rooting for the SEC's Auburn in the BCS Championship. The rest of the country was sort of pulling for Florida State only because FSU had the lone chance to end the SEC's glorious title run. This is what it's come to.

I've been accused of being a cheerleader for the SEC. Hey, I've been called worse. But how do you rip a conference whose only crime is having too much postgame confetti stuck in its hair? How do you criticize a league that won seven consecutive national championships and came within seventy-nine seconds of an eighth?

Answer? You can't.

T. J. Moe, a wide receiver for Missouri when the Tigers first joined the SEC in 2012, had it right about his new league when he told the *New Yorker*'s Reeves Wiedeman, "They say the girls are prettier, the air is fresher, and the toilet paper is thicker."

Right you are, Moe. They also say a thing or two about the players.

Everybody has a grudge against the SEC until they don't. When he was at Wisconsin, Badgers coach Bret Bielema proudly proclaimed, "We at the Big Ten don't want to be like the SEC in any way, shape or form." About ten months later, he ditched Madison for Arkansas and Woo Pig Sooie.

How do you feel about us now, Bret?

"This is the best conference in all of college athletics."

I couldn't have said it better myself.

A few days after Alabama won the 2009 BCS Championship, I was shopping in a Birmingham Wal-Mart when a stranger pulled up next to my cart. His cart was stuffed with Alabama football T-shirts, sweatshirts, jerseys and caps. He had cornered the market on crimson.

"Mr. Finebaum," he said proudly, "I am from Bangladesh. Today, I am an Alabama fan."

And I am a fan of the SEC—the land of championships, beauty queens, crisp autumn days and four-ply tissue.

I think Paul, when I've seen him and been around him,
he seems kind of quiet, conservative, kind of in the corner.
He comes across as a really shy person. But when
it's showtime, he fires it up.

—I-MAN

CHAPTER 2

This Isn't Live, Is It?

Saturday, August 31, 2013
Clemson, South Carolina

THE SEASON SKINNY: Alabama is No. 1 in both preseason polls and proves it by making Virginia Tech cry "Uncle!" in the opener, 35–10. . . . Five SEC teams are ranked in the top ten. . . . Per NCAA ruling, Johnny Manziel must sit out the first half of Texas A&M's season opener against Rice. . . . One Las Vegas sportsbook says that the money bet on Ohio State to win the BCS Championship is double that of any other team. . . . Auburn's odds to win the BCS have improved from 1,000/1 to 200/1.

It is 9:30 a.m. and my sweat is sweating.

I am in a brand-new suit and a nervously knotted tie, but more important, I am on the campus of Clemson University, and on an auxiliary TV stage, sitting next to the famed host of ESPN's *College GameDay*, Chris Fowler. Thousands of Tigers fans (with a dollop's worth of Georgia fans mixed in) are waving homemade signs and yelling like they're on Krispy Kreme sugar highs. What's in the drinking fountains here, water or 5-Hour Energy?

Clemson's cheerleaders, all pretty enough to win a Miss South Carolina contest, shake their orange-and-purple pom-poms just a few feet behind me, not far from their fellow Clemson students, apparently upset at my past ACC-bashing, who are shaking their fists at me.

It is my first-ever appearance as the newest "contributor" on the network's franchise show and, man, could I use a hug.

Scared? More like terrified. I feel like a guy making his first bungee jump off a bridge—except I've forgotten to double-check the bindings.

I'm not going to pretend that being on *GameDay* isn't a big deal to me. It is a bucket list type of accomplishment.

I spoke to my wife earlier in the morning.

"Are you excited about going on *GameDay*?" said Linda, who is a practicing doctor of internal medicine.

"I really am," I said.

"I hope you do well," she said. "If you bomb, I'll rescind my resignation with my medical group in Birmingham."

She was joking—I think. Linda had tendered her resignation because of our impending move from Birmingham to the Charlotte area, where my new ESPN studios are located.

Quietly, I pray. I do that a lot—before I get on planes, before I go on any show, including my own radio show. I close my eyes, take a few moments to reflect, to ask for help, to give me a sense of inner peace.

Hey, I'm not so proud that I can't use the help. I'm a big believer in faith, but I don't wear my spirituality on my sleeve. It's important to me, though. I want to do the right thing.

I'm not sure the higher powers are that interested in my *GameDay* debut. I am wearing makeup. My glasses are slightly askew. And Fowler, who has been hosting *GameDay* since 1990, is glancing at me with a bemused, let's-see-how-this-science-experiment-goes look on his face.

About two hours ago, I taped a *SportsCenter* segment from the *GameDay* set. It aired at 8:30, and afterward Lee Corso, the iconic former coach who has been holding court on the show and waving that No. 2 Ticonderoga pencil for twenty-five-plus years while saying, "Not so fast, my friend," pulled me aside in the *GameDay* meeting room.

"Paul, what's the problem?" he said.

"What do you mean, Coach?" I said.

"I just saw you on *SportsCenter*. You looked so serious. Paul, you're talking about college football. Have fun. And, most important, smile! When you smile, people don't get mad at you."

I'm not by nature someone who smiles. I think I was born with the facial elasticity of an IRS auditor.

But I'm trying to remember Coach Corso's advice as I take my place on the *GameDay* set for my 9:30 appearance. I grin nervously at Fowler, who reaches over, shakes my sweaty hand, and introduces me to America.

He asks me about Auburn's hiring of the team's former offensive coordinator, Gus Malzahn, who will be replacing Gene Chizik just two seasons after the Tigers won the 2010 BCS National Championship. How long, asks Fowler, will Auburn fans remain patient after the disastrous 3-9 season in 2012?

The words spill out of my mouth: Chizik was the worst coach to ever win a national championship . . . Before coaching his first game as a head coach, Malzahn has already turned the program around based on the strength of his staff hires, his recruiting efforts and his offensive schemes . . . Auburn's going to probably win seven or eight games in 2013.

I can see Fowler almost recoil.

Thirty minutes later, just after Fowler interviews Alabama coach Nick Saban by satellite, I'm back on the set. What are the Tide's chances of winning an unprecedented third consecutive national championship?

I start out reasonably enough, saying that the only thing that can stop Alabama is . . . Alabama—but I don't foresee a collapse.

So far, so good.

But then I can't help myself. I report that I have long considered Ohio State a possible successor to Alabama in the national title race, but have changed my mind after realizing the Buckeyes aren't good enough to finish in the upper division of the SEC.

"I think they'd rank five or six, at best," I tell America.

I almost feel the middle fingers pointed at me from Columbus, Ohio. And on set, I hear snickers and mocking laughter.

Desmond Howard, the former Heisman Trophy winner, says that a young SEC team could come along and shock everybody: Ole Miss.

Kirk Herbstreit, the former quarterback and team captain at Ohio State, warns that complacency could be Alabama's undoing in 2013.

And Coach Corso notes that the departure of senior placekicker Jeremy Shelley could be the difference in Bama's season.

I'm too nervous to care. I'm out of my depth, my comfort zone and, a part of me considers, maybe my mind.

The season before, I had hosted a local TV show from Birmingham that aired in Huntsville, Mobile, Dothan and Montgomery, and during the same time slot as *GameDay*. I was thrilled and honored to do it. Now I'm on one of the flagship ESPN shows? I've gone from being seen in parts of Alabama in 2012 to being seen nationwide in 2013.

When my two *GameDay* segments are finished, I feel like I've survived Navy SEALS training. If this is my one and only *GameDay* experience, then I'm going to enjoy every last moment of it. Exhilarated, exhausted, I climb the small set of metal stairs on the side of the main stage and watch Coach Corso make his headgear pick: Clemson or Georgia? Tigers or Dawgs?

If you want to watch somebody who enjoys himself, who doesn't treat college football as if it's the Battle of Dunkirk, then watch Lee Corso set up his headgear pick. He's a showman.

Coach Corso teases the crowd by saying that he is "done with dogs." The Clemson crowd cheers. Corso is on their side!

And then he isn't. Someone hands him a giant UGA mascot head. Then two bulldog puppies appear on the desk of the set.

I watch the whole thing unfold—the reaction from the sea of

Clemson orange, one of the puppies falling asleep on the desk, the natural camaraderie of Fowler, Coach and Herbstreit. This is college football personified. This would never happen in the NFL.

And then I realize I had taken Coach Corso's advice without knowing it.

How long had I been smiling?

Paul's extremely talented. I know, because I am too.

—JIM FROM TUSCALOOSA

CHAPTER 3

The SEC and Me—a Love Story

Tuesday, September 3, 2013

Charlotte, North Carolina

THE SEASON SKINNY: The final scheduled game between Notre Dame and Michigan at the Big House approaches. . . . The AP top ten: Alabama, Oregon, Ohio State, Clemson, Stanford, South Carolina, Texas A&M, Louisville, LSU and Florida State. . . . Bama receives fifty-eight of the sixty first-place votes, Ohio State and Clemson split the other two.

Former Alabama coach Ray Perkins, whose personality was so icy that you could enter a hypothermic state by sitting next to him, once said of me: "I've never seen anyone go so far in his profession on so little talent." That from a guy with a 74-90-1 career coaching record at Bama and the NFL.

Until I find a new house, I'm stuck living in one of those extended-stay hotels near the freeway, and thinking of Perkins. They have fresh chocolate chip cookies each night, but I miss my wife, who is still in Birmingham, where she'll stay all season, practicing medicine. I'm here in Charlotte practicing radio and TV. Not too much has happened to us in the last six months, except for my three new jobs, the new, intimate friends I've acquired at Charlotte's and Birmingham's respective TSA checkpoints, and this make-do crib near the interstate.

How did I ascend to such heights, you may be asking? How does a kid who never played a down of intramural flag football become the Mouth of the football South? How does a political science major wind up on the same *College GameDay* set as ESPN's four football horsemen: Fowler, Corso, Herbstreit and Howard? How does a fifty-something end up talking college football every day with ten-through-eighty-somethings, and occasionally with the Great Saban himself?

The answer is simple: I don't know. It's like asking who thought a comb-over was a good idea. Some things defy logic. I guess my career is one of them.

Well, for starters, Finebaum is a German name. It means, "Good tree." Of course, in some parts of the SEC and all parts of the Big Ten and ACC, Finebaum also means, "Squid feces."

In the old country, Finebaum is pronounced "Fine-ba-olm." Doesn't exactly roll off the tongue, does it?

My grade school teachers always called me "Fine-bomb," and it stuck. I got tired of correcting them. Years and years later, MSNBC's Rachel Maddow introduced me on her show as Paul "Finney-baum."

You also should know that my mother, Gloria, was the daughter of Romanian (on my grandfather's side) and Austrian (on my grandmother's) immigrants. Her father was a tailor, her mother a dressmaker. You can find their names somewhere in the Ellis Island archives. They didn't speak English when they arrived, but they learned. They worked hard and pushed their daughter hard. And the daughter grew up, got married, had a son named Paul, and pushed him hard too.

My father, Ben, was the son of a London insurance agent. His younger sister introduced him to my mom (the families lived in the same neighborhood) and after the marriage they eventually followed my uncle (an optometrist, like my dad) from New York to Tennessee in the mid-1950s. They had me not long after they arrived in Memphis. I'll never forget when my grandparents would come to visit us there. Afternoon tea was served promptly at 4 p.m., complete with scones and jam. It was all very British, very proper.

Keep calm and pass the cream, y'all.

I was a mutt, a fifty-fifty mix of the sensibilities of my mother, who believed in discipline and high expectations, and my father, who solved problems with a subtle intelligence and a gentle nature. From this, came me. I'm ambitious, but not in an overt, overpowering way. I'm understanding, but I won't be bullied. I'm a fan of humility, but I'm also proud of my accomplishments. I'll never win a bar fight, but I can win an argument. And I think that's a lot harder to do than throw a punch.

I have an older sister, Pam, who was born in New York on October 4, 1951, almost five years before I came along. On the day before Pam's birth, my mother was in the maternity ward listening to a program on the radio when she suddenly began screaming. The other soon-to-be-mothers in the ward craned their necks to watch as medical personnel rushed to my mom.

Was the baby on the way?

No, actually. My mother was a huge New York Giants fan and had been listening to the final baseball game of the regular season. When the Giants' Bobby Thomson hit the home run in the bottom of the ninth to beat the Brooklyn Dodgers—"The Giants win the pennant! The Giants win the pennant!"—my mom couldn't contain herself.

I'm not sure what she was happier about: giving birth to Pam the next day or Thomson giving birth to the Shot Heard 'Round the World.

I was a New York Yankees fan (surprise), but grew to root for the St. Louis Cardinals, the closest Major League franchise to Memphis. Their Double A team—the Chickasaws, then the Blues—played in town. In fact, I had a summer pass to Blues games and went to the ballpark almost every night.

Funny the things you can remember. "Let's get in the car and go so see a ball game," I can still hear my dad saying, casually, as we sat at the dinner table.

So we got in the car and drove to . . . Chicago. That's 533 miles from Memphis. And my jaw was probably on the car floorboard for the entire trip. I couldn't believe we were going to see the White Sox!

We didn't have PlayStation 4 back then. Video games hadn't been invented yet. There were no fantasy baseball leagues. Instead, we had Strat-O-Matic. We had the box scores in the newspaper. We had our imaginations. Sometimes, very rarely, we even had the real thing.

My father used to take me to St. Louis to see the Cards, too. We were there for the July 4, 1969, game between the Cardinals and Chicago Cubs. I've got it memorized: Fergie Jenkins pitched a 10-inning complete game to beat Bob Gibson, 3–1. And the game took just 2 hours and 32 minutes. These days, 2 hours and 32 minutes doesn't get you to the fourth inning.

Baseball was our family sport. Football, let alone college football, barely registered. I think a lot of kids in my generation grew up that way. The game consumed me. I knew all the players. Had all the cards. I played second base and the outfield on our Little League teams. OK, mostly just the outfield. I was terrible. But I loved the game.

What made baseball so special—and I know it's a bit of a Hallmark card cliché—is that I could share it with my father, and he could share it with me. It brought us closer together. It helped us become friends. Is it too corny to say that my father was my best buddy, that we did everything together? If so, I don't care. I loved him, respected him and admired him. He always saw the better angels in people.

I was fifteen when he died. A heart attack, his second in five years. After that, something changed in me, in who I was. The change was permanent and irreversible. I went from being a teenager with all those teenager concerns (girls, Clearasil, sports) to the man of the house.

His death didn't make sense then, and I'm not sure it makes sense forty-plus years later. One day your dad is walking in the door from work. The next day he's dead.

It was a difficult, emotional transition for my mom and me. She took a job as an office clerk at the IRS office in Memphis and did what she could to move the family forward, away from the grief and pain. Sure, she could be difficult. But who can blame her? I can't. We went to Memphis State basketball games together, even meeting the team at the airport late one school night after the Tigers had won at Louisville. On the way home, we stopped at IHOP for pecan waffles. I loved her for that.

But there's no nice way of saying this: my mother could be unbelievably difficult. If she were a car transmission, she'd have only one gear: Drive. She didn't believe in Neutral and she had no interest in Reverse.

My father's death instantly altered my plans for college, too. Most of my friends were going out of state, to Missouri, Georgia and especially to the University of Texas. That's where I wanted to go—to Austin. I wanted to be a Longhorn. Instead, I ended up at the other UT—the University of Tennessee. Given my family's financial circumstances, I didn't have much of a choice. Tuition was much lower as an in-state student and I was able to get some scholarship money to go there. But at least Knoxville was on the other side of the state, nearly four hundred miles away, so it would feel a *little* like going someplace different. And I definitely wanted different.

I missed my dad every day—still do. But I'm not sure I've ever missed him more than my first day at Tennessee in 1974. I flew from Memphis to Knoxville, caught a ride from the airport to campus, and then took my belongings (there wasn't much) to my drab dorm room, at drab Hess Hall, which looked like a Soviet Union apartment building during the reign of Khrushchev. My roommate hadn't checked in yet, so I started walking around the massive dorm. Everywhere I went dads and moms were bear-hugging their sons. I never felt so alone.

My freshman year at UT was mostly forgettable. It was like high school, but with ashtrays and all-you-can-eat buffets. I'd never seen so much food in my life. And free! I gained thirty pounds.

Gaining weight through fried foods and mystery meat isn't much of a college legacy. But something happened during the middle of my sophomore year that altered the course of my life. The randomness of it all still amazes me.

I was glancing through the student newspaper, the *Daily Beacon*, and saw a Help Wanted ad for a reporter position. I was bored, indifferent, uninspired by life. So on a whim I walked down to the bottom floor of the Communications College, a semicircular building located just across the street from Neyland Stadium, and submitted an application.

The first question an editor asked me was "Can you type?" The honest answer would have been "Yes—and if you believe that, I'm also dating Stevie Nicks." People who typed with their knees could type faster than me.

Instead, I mumbled something just loud enough that the editor thought I said, "Yes."

There was only one small problem with my budding journalism career: I couldn't write.

I'm not being modest; I truly didn't know how to write a newspaper story. It took me an epoch to type a paragraph, but even longer to structure it and find the right words to fill it. I didn't write for my high school newspaper. I hadn't taken any journalism classes before I applied for the *Beacon* job. I didn't know the Five Ws of journalism (Who, What, Where, When, Write Really Fast). I was lost.

Near the end of my sophomore year, I figured maybe it would all be a little easier if I wrote about sports, and so I approached the guy who ran that section. I'm not ashamed to admit it: I'm an opportunist. One of the first stories I wrote was about whether Bernard King, the gifted, otherworldly forward on the Tennessee basketball team (one half of "The Bernie and Ernie [Grunfeld] Show"), was going to leave early for the NBA after the 1976–77 season. More fun than writing the thing was watching other students read it—in my dorm, in my classes, in the cafeteria. Even my mom was proud.

Still, I was a political science major who was raised on politics— she probably thought my interest in sportswriting was a passing hobby. After all, our family dinners had been debate clubs with food. My mom worked at voting poll sites and even met with congressmen. I know this because she used to drag me along when I was eight or nine years old.

I was a politics junkie in high school. Given the choice between seats behind home plate to watch the Yankees in a World Series or seats on the floor at the Democratic or Republican conventions, I would have taken the conventions.

But when Watergate happened, I didn't go to the nearest parking garage to find my own Deep Throat, I wrote about how terrible the school basketball team was. Sports proved to be my escape. And then, inexplicably, it became something more. It became a possible career. Sorry, Mom.

I wasn't your typical sportswriter. I hadn't played high school sports or intramural sports. I didn't know a screen-and-roll from a hook-and-ladder. In retrospect, I was laughably naïve. I was covering the most influential and highly paid men in the state as if they hung on my every word, rather than vice versa. Bill Battle, Johnny Majors, Ray Mears. I challenged them all. I'd ask the indelicate question, write the confrontational (and sometimes juvenile) column. Mock. Tease. Criticize.

Remind you of a certain radio show?

I wanted to be an independent, different voice. I warred with Battle until he was fired in 1976. Thirty-seven years later he was named to succeed Mal Moore as athletic director at Alabama. We laugh about those UT days.

Cliff Wettig banned me from covering basketball games—he was the coach—after I wrote a mocking obituary of the program following another embarrassing Vols loss. More than a few frat boys and goobers in overalls gave me a hard time about being too anti-UT. They thought I should be a cheerleader with orange-and-white pom-poms, not a critic.

But the more I immersed myself in this strange jockish world, the more interested I became in the politics of sports.

The hiring and firing of coaches is political. The hiring and firing of athletic directors is political. Fund-raising is political. Recruiting is political. Campaigning for bowls, for rankings and for Heisman Trophies is political. Wooing the media is political. The conference office is political. The only difference is that the officials aren't elected. No one is. Big-time coaches are dictators.

I found myself fascinated by this combination of on-field sport and off-field intrigue. And I liked being the contrarian, trying to turn things upside down.

For years the SEC was America's best-kept football secret. Everybody else thought Ohio State–Michigan was a big deal, but we knew better. Bryant was at Alabama, having won three national titles in the 1960s and on his way to winning three more in the 1970s (Notre Dame followers don't acknowledge the 1973 UPI vote that, even though the Irish beat the Tide in the Sugar Bowl, has Bama finishing at No. 1, ahead of the Irish).

Johnny Majors, a former Tennessee star (he had finished second to Notre Dame's Paul Hornung in the 1956 Heisman balloting), returned to UT after coaching Pittsburgh to a national championship in 1976.

Vince Dooley (and a freshman running back named Herschel Walker) would lead Georgia to a national title in 1980.

You also had the coaching handoff from Frank Broyles to Lou Holtz at Arkansas. You had Doug Dickey at Florida. Charlie McClendon at LSU. Pat Dye would arrive at Auburn in 1981.

It was the beginning of a paradigm shift of college football power, from the Rust Belt to the Sun Belt. We knew Alabama-Auburn made that Big Ten rivalry look like a sorority pillow fight. But few people outside the South knew about the ferocity of the rivalry, or about the growing quality of the league. That's because the major television networks were infatuated with cramming Notre Dame, Oklahoma, USC, Texas, Nebraska and those Buckeyes and Wolverines down our throats every weekend.

When I was at Tennessee, I studied the weekly poll rankings as if they were a foreign-language requirement. I calculated how many SEC players should make the annual All-America teams (all of them). And it was never too early to think about which SEC team would play in what bowl.

I'm not going to say I saw the future of college football; I didn't. But I did recognize the passion and pride that SEC fans had for their particular brand of football. I saw the blind loyalty firsthand. I saw the power, even the insanity of their allegiances.

In other words, they were nuts—but in a good way. And I was a little nuts with them.

Byrant was a football god and he usually spent his third Saturday in October—at least, in the Bill Battle Era—beating Tennessee. Battle, a former Bama player, finished 1-6 against his old coach before getting forced out after the 1976 season.

I covered that 1976 loss to Bama at Neyland Stadium. I remember interviewing Vols offensive guard Mickey Marvin after the game. He muttered sadly, "Now I'm going to have to go through the rest of my life telling my children and my grandchildren that I never beat Alabama."

I had never seen Bryant in person until that moment he walked into the postgame interview room, which was splitting at the seams with reporters and camera crews. The great Bear . . . only a few feet away.

I pointed a tape recorder at him as he began to speak. His words of wisdom would be captured for posterity.

One problem: I couldn't understand a word he said. It was as if he were speaking in tongues. I went back to the press box to transcribe my tape and I still couldn't decipher Bryant's mumbling. So instead, I wrote a brooding, maudlin, Hemingway-esque column about walking into the rain after another Tennessee defeat—the rain that day in Knoxville serving as a metaphor for loss and death. I thought it was literature. It wasn't.

I earned my degree in political science and then, like all political science majors, decided to become . . . a sportswriter? I applied to dozens of different newspapers, including the *Washington Post*, the *New*

York Times, the *Boston Globe*, the *Los Angeles Times*, the *Chicago Sun-Times*—and then watched as the rejection letters poured in.

But not everyone turned me down. I had two offers: one from the *Shreveport Journal*, the afternoon paper in Shreveport, Louisiana, and the other from the *Bristol Herald Courier* in the sister cities of Bristol, Virginia, and Tennessee.

I took the job in Shreveport.

Shreveport is located near the northwest corner of the state. You can find it on a map alongside the Red River and near the Arkansas and Texas borders. It actually takes almost half the time to get to Dallas from Shreveport than it does to get to in-state New Orleans.

I drove from Knoxville to Shreveport in my college graduation present: a 1970s-something, used, powder blue Ford Maverick, which was such a good car that Ford quit making it in the 1970s. I didn't care. I loved that car, even though it had all the performance capabilities of a cinder block.

The *Journal* paid me $145 per week—before taxes. I thought it was all the money in the world. I lived in a duplex with an Iranian medical student who had escaped his country just before the fall of the shah of Iran.

The job itself was a good one for a kid just coming out of college. Because we were a medium-sized-circulation paper with a modest staff, we didn't have the luxury of being assigned single beats. So I helped cover LSU, the New Orleans Saints and the Dallas Cowboys. It was a terrific learning experience.

The downside? My checking account was on life support. So was my love life.

My girlfriend was from the Tri-Cities area, which includes Kingsport, Bristol and Johnson City. (Johnson City is where Steve Spurrier played high school football, by the way.)

My girlfriend had wanted me to take the job in Bristol, which would have been better for our relationship. But Shreveport was better for my career, so I chose my career. That didn't go over real well with the girlfriend.

Whatever money I could save, I would use to buy a plane ticket for my girlfriend. She'd visit me every two or three months. Then it became every four or five months. Then it became every six months.

One day I checked my mail at the office and there was a letter from her. A Dear Paul letter. These were the days when people actually sent letters, not e-mails.

I was devastated, distraught. I wanted to call her, but I didn't want to risk getting emotional while sitting in the middle of the sports department. Plus, this was a call that required privacy and time.

So I drove home in my powder blue Maverick and began piecing together what I would say to my girlfriend. I would win her back. I *had* to win her back. We were meant for each other—even if she didn't realize it.

I got home, rushed inside, picked up the phone to call her and got . . . nothing. The line was dead. The phone company had turned off my service. I was past due on the bill.

Now what? My mouth was dry. I took a glass out of the cabinet, held it under the kitchen faucet and got . . . nada. The water company had turned off my service. I was past due on the bill.

I sank into a chair, grabbed the remote control and aimed it at the TV. Zilch. The electric company had turned off my power. I was past due on that bill too.

So I sat in my tiny duplex apartment living room—alone, broke, desperate. My girlfriend had dumped me. My phone didn't work. I had no water. The electricity had been shut off. And, as an added bonus, I was working in Shreveport. This was my life.

I didn't really have any friends, with the exception of a young fellow reporter named Phil Rogers, who came to the paper about six months after I started.

Phil was from Denton, Texas, just north of Dallas, and when we could get away, he used to take me back home to visit his family. He basically took pity on me, and I've never forgotten the kindness.

Phil did OK for himself. He's become one of the best baseball writers in the country, a must-read at MLB.com.

One of the last stories I wrote during my fourteen-month stay in Shreveport was a non-sports feature about riding shotgun on a rig during an independent trucker strike. I rode scab for four straight days, seeing parts of this country I hope I never see again.

Driving a big truck is a tough way to make a living, and by the end of the trip I was checking my eyelids for pinholes (trucker slang for "I'm exhausted."). I actually wrote the story at 3 a.m. while parked in a truck stop.

In the story, I made a joke at the expense of Evansville, Indiana. As it turned out, the sports editor of the *Birmingham Post-Herald*—the guy offering me a job and a $20-a-week raise to leave Shreveport—was from Evansville. Lucky for me, he had a sense of humor.

The blue Maverick somehow got me from Shreveport to Birmingham, but its days were numbered. Not long after I arrived in Birmingham, a guy pulled up to me at a stoplight and said, "You better check that car of yours."

I said, "Really? Why's that?"

He gestured toward the rear of the Maverick. "'Cause you got fire coming out of your exhaust pipe."

And then he quickly drove away, presumably before my car exploded.

I traded in the Maverick for a brand-new Toyota Corolla, which was the size of a booth at Dreamland. But it had that new-car smell and, better yet, there were no flames spitting from the tailpipe like a Don Prudhomme dragster. It did 0 to 60 in a little less than a month, but I didn't buy it for horsepower. I bought it because—well, I'm not really sure why I bought that thing.

Birmingham was a good step for me. I was back in the SEC, back in my comfort zone. But I'm not sure Birmingham felt the same way about me.

First of all, I didn't look like a lot of the people in Birmingham. I was the antithesis of the late 1970s, early 1980s Sigma Chi frat boy. No khakis, penny loafers and button-down Brooks Brothers shirts for me. I had a beard, long hair (ah, the good old days) and John Lennon–wannabe glasses.

Second, the city itself—or more correctly, the city's racial history— unsettled me at times.

When I got to Birmingham in 1980, I still heard the N-word mentioned as casually as someone asking for the time of day. And part of me was sickened by the thought that racism and bigotry once ruled the day in Birmingham, a place Martin Luther King once described as the most segregated city in the country.

Police dogs. Fire hoses. Bull Connor. The bombings at the Sixteenth Street Baptist Church (which spawned the nickname "Bombingham").

It was a conflicted city in slow transition when I got there. It was a city trying to separate itself from its ignominious past. Now, decades later, I'm proud to say it is also a city that acknowledges its historic sins in a real and authentic way (visit Kelly Ingram Park, directly across from the Sixteenth Street Baptist Church, or the Birmingham Civil Rights Institute) and has learned from its mistakes.

I grew up in Southern cities. I lived in Memphis, the city where Dr. King was assassinated. I was taught at a very early age—and yes, I think racism and bigotry are learned behavior—that calling someone the N-word was unacceptable. MLK said it best: that he dreamed of a day when his children would not be judged by the color of their skin, "but by the content of their character." Those words have always stayed with me.

I remember the April 4, 1968, night my father walked in from work and said he had heard the bulletin of King's murder. We turned on the radio and listened to the sorrowful news.

It was traumatic for me, because even as a kid I was a student of history and had studied Dr. King's "I Have a Dream" speech. I simply couldn't understand why someone would kill a man who preached peace.

He was shot on a Thursday. The following Monday there was going to be a march in his honor. I wanted to attend, but my mother wouldn't let me—not because she didn't support the march, but because it was a volatile time, filled with anger, frustration and, in some cases, retribution.

I covered college football, of course, for the *Post-Herald*. During that 1980 season, there was an African-American quarterback at Auburn named Charles Thomas. In fact, Thomas was the program's first-ever African-American quarterback.

Maybe that doesn't sound like a big deal now, but thirty-plus years ago it didn't play too well in the South. There was still a feeling that black players weren't "equipped" to handle the position—so went the conventional, racist thinking at the time.

Auburn lost at home to Tennessee, 42–0, early that season and afterward in the locker room, Thomas calmly described how he had been booed and called the N-word by Tigers fans.

At the time, Walter Lewis, the first-ever African-American quarterback to play for Bryant, was a freshman at Alabama. The debate always came up: why were there so few African-American quarterbacks in the major college game? To me the answer was obvious: because there were so few coaches willing to stand up for what was right.

I wrote about Thomas's experiences at Auburn, and the column wasn't well received by our readers. But it was an issue that was important to me, and at every chance I was going to address it through my column.

To Birmingham's credit—to the South's credit—the overt racism has subsided. I'm not naïve enough to think racism doesn't still exist there. But the Birmingham I knew in 1980 isn't the Birmingham I've grown to love over the years. It has come a long way.

In those days, newspapers were still king and the Internet was still wearing braces and a retainer. If you were a sportswriter, you didn't dream of writing for a Web site. I'm not even sure the term had been invented yet.

No, you wanted to work for the regal *New York Times*, the gloriously over-the-top *Boston Globe*, which treated sports like one of the seven sacraments. You wanted to be at the big papers, where the fiercest newspaper wars were being fought with the sports pages as weapons. You wanted to be at a paper that mattered.

I was in Birmingham, Alabama, at a morning newspaper that was No. 2 in a two-paper market. Not long after I started working in Birmingham, I got a call from the *Nashville Banner*. They were just kicking the tires. They didn't have a specific job offer for me, but there was some level of interest. They said they'd get back to me.

And about a year after I'd been at the *Post-Herald*, an editor at the *Philadelphia Journal* called me. The upstart *Journal* was trying to compete against the city's more established and respected *Inquirer* and *Daily News*.

I didn't know anything about the *Journal*, but I did know it wasn't in Birmingham. And I knew that I had a better chance of making a newspaper name for myself by working for a bigger East Coast newspaper in a huge sports town than I would in Birmingham.

And the *Journal* offered me more than twice what I was making at the *Post-Herald*.

But as much as I liked the higher salary, the bigger emphasis on sports and the larger market, the *Philadelphia Journal* was no *New York Times*. And about three months later—long after I turned them down—it wasn't even the *Philadelphia Journal* anymore. The paper folded in December 1981 after four years of financial losses. I would have been out of a job, just like the other 150-plus employees.

And remember the *Nashville Banner* call I got? The *Banner* would eventually fold too. I was coveted by papers with no future, which was sort of the story of my career.

My mom, of course, was unimpressed by my career path. She thought I should have been the junior senator from Tennessee by then, not a sports reporter in Birmingham. But she couldn't hide her pride when I called her up and told her I had just won first place in the annual Associated Press Sports Editors competition. I had done an investigative series (with the help of our sports editor, Bill Lumpkin) on Bobby Lee Hurt, an Alabama high school basketball star who was alleged to have received cash payments while at Huntsville's Butler High School.

The series won a handful of prestigious awards and attracted the attention of some much larger newspapers, such as the *Philadelphia Inquirer*. The series also resulted in a libel suit against the paper—and me, among others.

Unlike the *Philly Journal*, the *Inquirer* was a cornerstone newspaper. It was engaged in a spirited newspaper war, and it wanted me as one of its soldiers. It was the big leagues. In fact, the *Inquirer* wanted to hire me to cover Major League Baseball.

This was the biggest moment of my career. I was going to cover baseball in one of the great baseball towns. My bags were packed. I was counting the minutes until I got on the plane Monday morning.

And then my phone rang at three o'clock on Sunday afternoon.

It was the *Inquirer* sports editor. Something had come up, he said. Don't bother coming to Philadelphia for the interview. He'd be in touch.

I was numb, devastated. The best moment of my career had become the worst. Somebody in management had decided they weren't going to hire a guy who was in the middle of a lawsuit.

That lawsuit not only cost me the *Inquirer* job, but it scared away several other papers that had contacted me about possible jobs.

About six months later, we won the lawsuit, but it didn't matter. I never got another offer from a major paper.

It was one of those moments that changed my life. I didn't realize it at the time, but not getting that job may have been the best thing that happened to me. It's like that Garth Brooks song: *Some of God's greatest gifts are unanswered prayers . . .*

At the time, it was a massive ego blow. I was distraught, inconsolable. I had it all planned out: a year or two at the *Inquirer* and then I'd move up the interstate to New York and the *Times*. My career would be made.

When I didn't get the *Inquirer* job, it was as if my self-esteem had been hijacked. I went into a medium-sized personal tailspin. I brooded. I became dark, or at least murky. I had only the wisps of a social life. I was the kind of guy who would read Camus or Kafka in an unpainted room with a single, bare bulb hanging from the ceiling.

It's like that line in *When Harry Met Sally* when Billy Crystal says, "When I buy a new book, I read the last page first. That way, in case I die before I finish, I know how it ends. That, my friends, is a dark side."

Not long after the *Post-Herald* won the lawsuit, I was promoted to sports columnist. So I worked even harder. I was Sabanesque without knowing it. I never got too high, never got too low. OK, maybe more low than high.

Early in my career, I was supremely confident. I really thought I was a better reporter than anyone else. If there had been an NFL Draft for reporters, I'd have considered myself a top-five pick.

But little by little, as your dreams don't pan out, you reevaluate. You lower your expectations. You convince yourself that this is all life has to offer—and you're OK with that. You move on, but I'm not sure you move forward.

It probably didn't help that I went after Bear Bryant in print, which *nobody* did. But sorry, how does Alabama let Bessemer's Bo Jackson go to *Auburn*?

You could call me a lot of things back then, but "Bryant lapdog" wasn't going to be one of them. And to be honest, I was trying to make a name for myself, even if that name was seemingly going to be confined to the greater Birmingham area.

My fellow sportswriters resented me. The Alabama fans hated me. I got death threats. Someone left a message on my voice mail at work and said: "You are going to die." And then he detailed exactly how he was going to kill me.

It didn't scare me. First of all, I died every time I had to write a column on deadline. Second, I'd already been sued a few times and had endured more than a few court trials. At that point death threats were the least of my worries.

The police tapped my phone for about six months, but the guy never called back. Maybe I wasn't worth the trouble.

Don't misunderstand me about Bryant. I respected him and admired his accomplishments. He was a symbol. If you lived in Alabama, he was the leading cause of puffed-out chests and excessive bragging. Bryant made Alabamans proud—and that was no small thing in the context of those times.

He was clever. When you visited Bryant in his office, his desk—and he—seemed to tower over you. That's because, I swear, the legs of the guest chairs had been cut down, so you'd almost have to peer over the top of his desk to see him. It was a great home-field advantage.

During the 1981 and 1982 Alabama seasons, I had sort of a direct BearPhone line to Bryant. I would call him every Monday morning and he would answer a half dozen or so questions as part of a weekly package in our sports section.

This was heady stuff for a guy only a couple years out of college. I would try to act nonchalant during my interviews with him, but my heart was beating as fast as hummingbird wings. Plus, I was worried that I wouldn't be able to translate his mumblings.

But Bryant was fine. In fact, he was clearer and more coherent after a loss than he was after a victory. And even though I had taken my shots at him in the paper, he never held it against me. I think he was amused by me, much like a Doberman is amused by a yapping Chihuahua. Perhaps he respected the idea that someone would challenge his decisions. Maybe I'm reading too much into it and he was just too old to give a damn.

I'm not going to lie: it was pretty fun to go to lunch every Monday with friends and casually mention that I had just spoken with the Bear. Bryant and I didn't have a close relationship, but there was a level of trust. He was larger than life; I was a virtual nobody. And yet he treated me with a kindness and respect that I've never forgotten and, at times, probably didn't deserve.

We spoke one-on-one twenty-two times during those seasons. How lucky was that? I wish I had saved those interview notebooks as mementos.

In 1981, Bryant won just nine games, only the second time in the previous eleven seasons he had failed to lead Bama to at least 10 victories. In 1982, his final year at Alabama, the Tide started 5-0, climbed to No. 2 in the rankings and then lost four of its last six regular-season games, including losses to Tennessee and Auburn. It was Bryant's worst record since 1970.

He was sixty-nine and earned $100,000 a year—or about $7 *million* less than Saban will make in 2014. When he announced his retirement from coaching about two and a half weeks later—the December 29 Liberty Bowl in my hometown of Memphis would be his final game— Bryant said, "I'm a tired old man, but I'll never get tired of football." And then the tired old man who had won 322 games in his career said, "In my opinion they deserve better coaching than they've been getting from me this year."

The plan was for Bryant to remain as Alabama's athletic director. New York Giants coach Ray Perkins, a former star receiver at Bama, would replace Bryant on the sidelines.

Bryant's resignation announcement affected me in a personal and professional way. I was only a few years into my sportswriting career, but I kept thinking, "It's never going to be this good again. I'm never going to be able to cover a story that tops this."

Here I was, sitting in the same room where one of the greatest coaches of all time was calling it quits, and I was mildly depressed by the news. Part of it was selfishness, and part of it was the realization that the great Bear Bryant was really leaving. It was truly the end of an era. Covering anybody else after the Bear would feel so . . . well, small.

Bryant looked older than he was. He had a sense of weariness about him. But he was still a big man physically and he had a John Wayne–like presence that commanded attention. I've seen presidents enter a room, watched celebrities and famous people make their entrances, but nothing compares with the effect Bryant had on a football audience.

Bama beat Illinois in the Liberty Bowl on a raw, cold Memphis night. You could see that Bryant didn't look well.

I spoke with him two weeks later about a magazine piece I was working on. He didn't sound great, but like everyone else, I figured he had been worn down by the difficult season. He would rest, recharge and report to work as Bama's athletic director.

Instead, he fooled us all and died. We didn't think that was possible. The Bear . . . dead? Wasn't he supposed to live forever?

The funeral service was in Tuscaloosa and the burial was in Birmingham. Former Ohio State coach Woody Hayes was at the service. So was former Arkansas coach Frank Broyles, and the legendary Eddie Robinson of Grambling State, whom I had grown to admire while working in Shreveport. In fact, anybody who was anybody in the football world was there.

There was an official motorcade made up of the hearse that carried Bryant's casket, as well as six buses filled with dignitaries and football heads of state. After that it was like a Mad Max movie, with every grieving Alabama fan lining up in his or her car to follow the motorcade to Birmingham. Imagine the Oklahoma Land Rush, but with smog-spewing AMC Alliances, Oldsmobile Supremes and Chevy Caprices revved up at the start line.

I bogarted my way into the very end of the funeral procession, just after the last official car had passed and just before the state trooper escort closed the gap. My assignment that day for the *Post-Herald* wasn't complicated: describe the scene.

An estimated half million people lined Interstate 59 as we made the drive. Dozens and dozens of eighteen-wheelers had pulled to the side of the freeway to let the procession go through. You could see the drivers standing next to their rigs, their weathered hats placed over their hearts.

Fans lined the overpass bridges. You could see the signs: "God Needs an Offensive Coordinator." Or, "We Miss You, Bear."

Grown men wept—and I was one of them. Yes, me, the guy who had taken more than a few swings at Bryant in the paper. The guy who swore he didn't have a soft spot for college football coaches. The guy who had been angry at the world ever since his own dad had died.

But as I drove and spoke into my tape recorder to describe the scene, I was overwhelmed by the outpouring of love toward Bryant. Tears somersaulted down my cheeks. I choked up. I couldn't help it.

I guess it was at that exact moment that I realized that football was bigger than life in Alabama. Thirty-plus years later, those memories still stick with me.

I'm not saying I softened my stance toward the program, but I began to look at Bama football differently than I had before. I think I had begun to understand how that program was embedded in the hearts and souls of those who followed those Bama teams. And Bryant had been their patriarch.

I'm not sure 500,000 folks would line the interstate if Saban spun in tomorrow. He hasn't been at Alabama as long as Bryant, he hasn't won as many games and his back story isn't built for movie scripts (the Bear had the Junction Boys at Texas A&M, he wrestled a bear when he was thirteen, he was the eleventh of twelve children and was raised on an Arkansas farm).

Bryant led Alabama out of the football wilderness. He won six national championships. He was beloved, revered, worshipped. He had one of the most memorable nicknames and wardrobes in American sports history. I say this in the most admiringly, nonsexist way possible, but go to any Alabama game these days and you'll see women and coeds wearing skintight houndstooth-patterned skirts with cowboy boots. So I guess the Bear does live on forever.

I had grown to admire Bryant for lots of different reasons. It isn't often you meet someone who transcends an entire sport, who is a legend in the real sense of the word.

For whatever reason, Bryant's death caused me to reevaluate my own career arc. I liked sportswriting, but I'm not sure I loved it. I wanted to try something different—but what?

Then one day in 1984 I got a call about a part-time job. The salary? Exactly $100.

The job? Radio host.

I know this guy from the South Side of Chicago. He runs a national corporation. He's a Notre Dame season ticket holder. He said to me, "You know what? I want to punch that Finebaum guy in the face. I want to turn his show on too, but I want to punch him in the face."

—JEFF FROM CHICAGO

CHAPTER 4

If Only Johnny Football Would Call the Show

Saturday, September 7, 2013
Birmingham, Alabama

THE SEASON SKINNY: Michigan Men beat the Domers. . . . You are looking live at Brent Musburger and Eminem in the Michigan Stadium booth. . . . An SEC firsta wedding ceremony/tailgate is held near Neyland Stadium, where the happy couple receives a wedding gift from the Vols: a Tennessee rout of Western Kentucky.

Can I give you some advice?

If you call my radio show—and I love it when you do—have something to say. Don't be this person:

Me: You're on the air.
You: I am?
Me: Yes, you are. What's on your mind?
You: Hey, Paul.
Me: Hey.
You: How you doin'?
Me: Fine.
You: That's good.

No, it isn't. It's radio death. It's pound-my-head-against-a-studio-soundboard exasperating. It's on to the next caller.

I'm a patient man. I like people. I like callers, even the ones who'd like me to eat the forest berries from *The Hunger Games*.

But don't call the show and ask me how I'm doing. I'm doing great. I'm happily married. I have the loyalty of a fine dog. My socks match. What more could I ask for?

If I want to make idle chitchat, I'll talk to the parking lot attendant. If I want to talk college football, I'll talk to you. But you have to actually say something about college football.

I have the most caller-driven show in the country. We might not have the best guests, but we have the best callers. We're the *American Idol* of call-in shows. Call us and there's a chance you can become a star.

Ask Tammy. Ask Jim from Tuscaloosa. I-Man. Legend. Darriel in Columbus. Charles Allen Head. Phyllis from Mulga. Jeff from Chicago. Jim from Crestwood. Robert from Waterloo. I could list another dozen go-to callers who make a difference.

I don't want you to be *on* the show. I don't want you to be *part* of the show. I want you to *be* the show.

We are the show where the average guy can be heard—the working stiff who can't get to the stadium; the guy who's an SEC fan, but can't get a ticket; the guy who when he tailgates grills hot dogs, not bison burgers from a boutique butcher. We're like the old TV show *Cheers*, where everybody knows your name.

The regulars get it. They don't just listen to the show. They challenge me. They call me out. They call anybody and everybody out. And they know the unwritten rules of *The Paul Finebaum Show*.

Such as:

Don't call during bowl season and ask who I like in the Australian Open. Don't ask who I like in the Australian Open in *any* season. I don't care.

I don't care about the World Series. I quit caring about baseball when the games started taking longer than a flight to Norway.

I don't care about the PGA's precious FedExCup. The only thing I want FedEx to do is deliver my package before 2 p.m.

I don't care that the Kansas City Chiefs have won three in a row. Or that Kevin Durant scored 46. Or that Man U did whatever Man U does.

I care about college football. I care about the SEC. I even care about those other conferences that will never be the SEC.

You want to know about the Australian Open? Go ask the McEnroes. The World Series? I suggest e-mailing Tim Kurkjian. Golf? Contact Eldrick. The NFL? See if John Clayton and Slayer will take your call. The NBA? Someone from the Van Gundy family. Soccer? Got me.

I can talk about other things—and there are times when I love doing that. But I *know* college football. So do my callers.

Tammy is an Auburn fan so outrageous, so politically incorrect and so proudly redneck that there are people who actually think she's an actress paid to come on the show. That she's playing a character—has to be.

She's real, all right—and loud, obnoxious, inappropriate and generally wonderful. I've had to ban her from the show on occasion, but she always makes a triumphant return. Tammy can't stand me most days, but she has a love affair with the SEC and Auburn. I've heard her say, "Down here in the Deep South, we're all about football. It's like a marriage—you attract a man to you by heart, soul and passion. Football down here has all of that."

When Alabama played in the Rose Bowl for the 2009 BCS Championship, I jokingly had asked Tammy if she wanted to come out to Los Angeles, and said I would take her to the Polo Lounge at the world-famous Beverly Hills Hotel, the same hotel frequented in the past by the likes of Howard Hughes, the Beatles, John Wayne, Henry Fonda and the Duke and Duchess of Windsor.

Tammy wasn't interested.

"I ain't stayin' at no Beverly Hill motel," she said.

But for all her bluster and bravado, her most poignant moment came when she called the show in the wake of the Penn State/Jerry Sandusky scandal and talked about being raped as a child. It was chilling, compelling and intensely personal. Nobody, and I mean nobody, could ever think Tammy was an actress after that day.

Jim from Tuscaloosa is the one caller who can literally change the direction of the show. If I see his name on the monitor, he immediately gets on the air. I could be interviewing President Obama, but I would bump him for Jim from Tuscaloosa. He is the human safety net for the show and probably the best caller in the history of our program.

There is no gray area with Jim from Tuscaloosa. He can be cantankerous, sometimes venomous, but he always has an opinion. He buries you with logic. He'll go months without calling the show if he thinks we haven't met his sports talk standards. He isn't afraid to rip callers, guests or me. Jim from Tuscaloosa can hold a grudge. And what other caller insists he was a better hitter than Ted Williams? Only Jim from Tuscaloosa.

Phyllis from Mulga lives for Alabama football, and God help the person who crosses her. She screams and hollers at anybody who criticizes her precious Tide. We gave her a lifetime ban after one of her more inappropriate outbursts, but she appealed the ruling. So we held an on-air trial (Phyllis was supplied with a show-appointed defense attorney) and her ban was reversed.

You grow fond of these folks. In November 1996, Phyllis was diagnosed with lung cancer. Surgeons at St. Vincent's Hospital in Birmingham removed the bottom lobe of her left lung.

When she was moved from intensive care to a regular hospital room, I went to visit her (a friend had alerted me to the situation). We had never met in person.

She was sitting on the side of the bed, a monstrous-looking oxygen apparatus attached to her face like an elephant trunk. It was there to help drive oxygen into her lung.

I said hello. For a change, Phyllis was at a loss for words.

She removed the oxygen tubing.

"I'm so sorry I look like this," she said.

"Don't you dare apologize for that," I said. "I just wanted to come and see you, and give you mine and Linda's best."

It was the least I could do. Phyllis would spend nine days in that hospital. But when she got out and called our show again, her voice, lungs and love of Bama football were all in working order.

Former Auburn coach Pat Dye is a piece of work—and also a show regular. When he was coaching, I'm fairly certain Dye used to despise me. He still might, but he hides it better.

In the locker room before a 1983 game at Tennessee, Dye actually read a couple of my columns to his team (I had questioned the Tigers' chances of winning at UT). Afterward, when Auburn had beaten the Vols, 37–14, Dye had asked me to stand up during the postgame press conference. So I stood up and Dye said grandly, "Here's the man who won us the game."

Shane from Centerpoint was one of our favorites. He died on December 1, 2011, after a long battle against lung cancer. We devoted the next day's show entirely to Shane and played a collection of his best calls. Under normal circumstances we would have built the show around the SEC Championship between LSU and Georgia, which was going to be played the next day. But remembering Shane was the right thing to do. We had so many people call in with their own favorite moments of Shane's appearances. It was like everyone was family.

Shane was a huge Bama fan who once reported a supposed Auburn recruiting violation to the NCAA. When an NCAA official asked him to identify himself, he said, "Shane from the Finebaum show."

One year he was hanging out with us at our SEC Media Days broadcast table when Saban showed up for a prearranged interview. Shane jumped up, stuck out his hand as if he were part of the crew and said, "Hey, Nick, Shane from Centerpoint."

The show mattered to Shane, and Shane mattered to us. I gave the eulogy at Shane's funeral and was honored to do so.

Anyway, nobody wants to listen to me for four hours. *I* don't want to listen to me that long.

Too many radio hosts fall in love with their own voices. I'm in love with our callers.

For example, there's Smokey, who called us from the hospital after suffering a heart attack. The on-air conversation:

> Me: Smokey, are you telling me that you're listening to the show while you're having a heart attack?
>
> Smokey: Yes, sir, I am. That's stupid, I know . . . They told me I got to hang up the phone, Paul.
>
> Me: Before you hang up . . . you're in the ER getting an EKG, but you're calling us?
>
> Smokey: Because I love you, Paul.

Aww.

There's a nationally known radio host—I've been a huge fan of his for years—who once asked me, "Why the f— do you talk to these crazy people?" And as soon as he said it, that was the line of demarcation. I talk to them because I can't get every national big-hitter guest like he can. But more important, I talk to them because nine times out of ten they're more interesting, more provocative, more down-to-earth than nine out of ten national big-hitter guests. Give me the choice between a great call and a great guest, and I'll take the great call every time.

They share their lives with us. They open their souls to us. Is it nuts sometimes? Sure. Do they occasionally violate FCC rules and the rules of good taste with what they say? (E.g., Glen from Forest, Louisiana, a die-hard LSU fan, called in after a Tigers loss to say his team had played "like a bunch of queer little boys." I later asked him if his wife was an LSU fan. "Aw, hell, yeah," he said. "I'd divorce her if she wasn't.") But I will never apologize for giving the Glens, the Smokeys, the Legends, I-Mans, Jims, Tammys, Shanes, Charles Allen Heads and Phyllises a place where they can vent. Plus, I remember a time when we were lucky to get ten people to *listen* to the show, much less call in. So I don't take any of them for granted.

One of our regulars I've given my cell phone number (which, come to think of it, might not have been the smartest thing I've ever done). One of them I've taken out to lunch. One of them I've flown all the way to Iowa to visit.

His name is Robert Fisher—or "Robert from Waterloo," as he is known on the show.

Robert is a thirty-five-year-old, wheelchair-bound college football fan who has cerebral palsy. He calls our show every day and always opens the conversation with, "Hey, what's up, buddy?" He thinks we're doing him a favor by taking his call. If only he knew it's the other way around.

Sometimes you run into a story that really matters. Robert matters.

His father, an Army veteran who had worked at the John Deere plant in Waterloo, Iowa, for thirty years before retiring, told me that even though he dearly loved his son, he was sometimes frustrated that Robert couldn't play sports. So some friends of mine arranged for Robert and his parents to come to Tuscaloosa for an Alabama–Ole Miss game. Before the game, we were at the campus quad and people began to recognize me—but even more so, began to realize that Robert was indeed "Robert from Waterloo."

Alabama fans spontaneously began to line up in front of Robert as if it were an organized book signing. The line stretched long and far. People wanted his autograph. They wanted to take a photo with him. Standing to the side was Robert's dad, who had a smile on his face as wide as a Bryant-Denny Stadium concourse.

I heard Robert's dad turn to his wife and say in a soft, shaky voice, "That's my boy."

He later told me it was the proudest moment of his life. Mine, too.

So to the national radio host who asked why I talk to these "crazy" people, well, Robert is why.

I've been lucky. Our callers are their own three-act plays and our guests have helped elevate the quality of the show. The interview I once did with novelist Pat Conroy, one of the great American writers of our time, remains a favorite. It was scheduled for ten minutes but lasted an hour. I'm not sure we even mentioned sports.

Not every guest appearance works out. Johnny Unitas, one of the NFL legends of my generation, provided the most awkward moment of my radio career. I made a good-natured crack about his iconic crew cut and I don't think he said another word during the "interview."

New York Yankees legend Don Larsen was on the show for one of those hurried promotional interviews, and it was a disaster.

"Don, let's talk about your perfect game," I said, referencing his Game Five masterpiece in the 1956 World Series.

"I'm tired of talking about my perfect game," he snapped.

The interview quickly ended. I mean, what were we supposed to talk about, his imperfect games?

Dee Snider, the lead singer for the heavy metal band Twisted Sister, came on the show in 2000. He supposedly was trying to distance the band from then–Atlanta Braves relief pitcher John Rocker, who was under severe public criticism for a variety of alleged knuckleheaded xenophobic and homophobic comments made in a *Sports Illustrated* piece. Turns out that one of Rocker's favorite songs was Twisted Sister's "I Wanna Rock." The Braves played it on the stadium loudspeaker every time he entered the game.

Snider had basically issued a cease-and-desist order to the Braves. He didn't want them to use the song until Rocker explained his controversial comments to the band.

Let's just say I had my doubts about the sincerity of Snider's demands. In fact, I told him on the air that I thought the whole thing was a publicity stunt.

Said Snider: "Publicity stunt? I'll tell you what's not a publicity stunt: when I come down there and kick your ass."

Here's the thing about hair bands: they wear metal studs and talk big, but I'm not sure any of them know how to fight. Maybe Snider was going to kick my ass with a blow-dryer. All I know is that he never made good on his threat.

We have all sorts of people on our show, including coaches, of course. Coaches think my callers are insane. And maybe some of the callers do have several screws loose. So what? Coaches aren't exactly the most well-balanced group of people you'll ever meet. Florida's Will Muschamp looks like he's going to have an aneurism on the sideline. LSU's Les Miles is capable of saying anything—and often does. Same goes for Steve Spurrier at South Carolina. Auburn's Gus Malzahn sleeps four hours a night and is consumed by football the other twenty. Mark Stoops *wanted* to coach at Kentucky. Kevin Sumlin happily climbed aboard the Mad Tea Cup ride that is Johnny Football. James Franklin thought Vanderbilt was a good job. At this very moment, Ole Miss's Hugh Freeze is probably out recruiting at KinderCare because of a pre-schooler's "measurables." Alabama's Saban is wound so tight during the season that he needs instructions on how to laugh. The 2013 season will be Mark Richt's thirteenth at Georgia—and he keeps coming back for more fan abuse.

And I haven't even mentioned some of the characters in the other conferences: Mike "I'm Forty, I'm a Man" Gundy, Bobby Petrino, Mike Leach, Bo Pelini, Charlie Weis, Lane Kiffin, to name a few.

I love it when coaches say, "I don't read the sports section and I don't listen to talk radio."

Guess what? They read sports sections and they listen to talk radio. And if they don't, someone they know does and tells them all about it.

The coaches can roll their eyes at some of our callers. But if their players cared half as much about their teams as my callers did, they'd have better records.

My radio show on WJOX in Birmingham had a heart attack on Monday, January 21, 2013. We were alive at 2 p.m., dead at 6 p.m. There were no goodbyes, no nothing. On Monday I had a show that could be heard locally and nationally (thank you, SiriusXM), on Tuesday I didn't. My contract had expired.

I didn't know what to do Tuesday. It was two o'clock—the time I'd normally be in the studio—and I was at home sitting with the dog. The phone rang every ten minutes. Friends called. Lawyers called. Reporters called. It got me through the afternoon.

The next day, Wednesday, I was lost. I had lunch with my wife. I got a haircut. I walked the dog. People looked at me during lunch as if there had been a death in the family.

On Thursday I spoke at the Greater Gardendale Chamber of Commerce. Short of a colonoscopy (which I actually had a few weeks later), there wasn't anything I dreaded more than that public appearance. There were reporters and camera crews waiting for me. And there was nothing I could say about my situation. My lawyers had instructed me to issue a "no comment" if asked about my contract situation with WJOX.

"Since I've had nothing to do the last three days," I told the audience, "I've prepared a four-hour speech."

It got a laugh.

I joked about needing a job, so the Jefferson County Commission later offered me work as a sewer worker. Good benefits package, by the way.

I became a professional lunch-goer. I became a professional phone talker, mostly to lawyers who were trying to negotiate me out of a three-month broadcast ban. I became a sad tale, with a stranger coming up to me in a men's clothing store and saying, "Hey, I'm really sorry you lost your job." At a Birmingham gas station, a guy walked up to me and said, "Man, I just want to hug you."

I had friends offer to give me part-time work. I'm not sure what that would have entailed—clearing wooded brush, cleaning their crawl spaces, babysitting—but I took a pass.

Oddly enough, I didn't miss doing the show. I missed the callers, but not the physical act of doing the show. I had mentally prepared myself not to do the show for a while as the lawyers determined my future.

Wait, I take that back. There were two days in particular that I wished I had had a show. One was March 30, 2013, the day that Alabama athletic director Mal Moore died.

I truly believe Mal Moore will be remembered in the same breath as Saban and Bear Bryant. He was that important.

He played at Bama, coached at Bama and then oversaw the football renaissance and ensuing dynasty of Bama. He was part of ten football national championships at Bama. I understand why there are statues of coaches at Bama, but Mal ought to have one too.

I joked with him the last time I saw him. I was hosting an event in late January commemorating the thirtieth anniversary of Bryant's death. And when I introduced Mal—and I obviously had no idea at the time that he was sick—I cracked wise about his legacy, saying that he wouldn't be remembered as the man who had been Bear Bryant's trusted assistant coach, or as the man who had been part of all these national titles, but that he would be forever remembered this way: "Mal Moore, comma, the man who hired Nick Saban."

He had roared with laughter that night. But I was only half-kidding. Mal revived Alabama football because he wouldn't take no for answer. His patience and his persistence when it came to romancing Saban is a large part of his professional legacy.

I knew he was having physical difficulties. Before the national championship game against Notre Dame, we had walked slowly around the Sun Life field together. I had asked him the same thing I always asked him: "How you feeling? What are you eating? You doing well?"

His whole family was there. I joked with his daughter and said, "I'm trying to get Mal to eat right." And she had laughed and said, "Good luck."

He hadn't looked well. He told me on the field that he had had shortness of breath. A heart condition was the cause.

I saw him three and a half weeks later and he still didn't look well. I just assumed he was still dealing with heart troubles.

Mal was taken to the medical facility at Duke University in Durham, North Carolina. I had talked to a friend of his, asking if I could visit with Mal when I was there for an upcoming speech in nearby Chapel Hill.

I never got the chance. Three days later, at age seventy-three, he died of pulmonary disease (he also had needed a lung transplant).

Thinking back on that night at the BCS Championship, I remembered seeing Dr. Robert Witt, the former president of Alabama who had approved Saban's hiring in 2007. "I'm just so happy for Mal," Witt had said in the waning moments of Bama's victory against Notre Dame.

Perhaps Witt knew the true extent of Mal's illness.

Mal was the perfect complement to Saban. The Alabama coach didn't like having a boss, but he could pass stuff along to Mal that he didn't want to deal with. Mal was a former coach, a gentle man who understood the demands of Saban's position. He wasn't some high-strung, forty-five-year-old MBA trying to tell him what to do. Mal let Saban do his job.

Mal was truly beloved. Even though he had died months earlier, Mal got a standing ovation at the Bama Coaches Caravan after a video tribute was played in his memory. The fans loved him. And always will.

I wish I could have dedicated a show in his honor. He was deserving of a four-hour retrospective and much more.

I wish I could have done a show on April 15, 2013: The Boston Marathon Bombings. I was at home when the news broke. The bombings happened only a few minutes before my show would have normally gone on the air.

It's just a radio show, but I would have liked to have helped in any small way a radio show can help. Because I believe this show does connect with people in ways that go beyond who wins or loses a college football game.

That certainly happened in the aftermath of the sixty-two deadly tornadoes that ripped through Alabama in late April 2011, killing 253 people. Rather than just call the show, Randy Owen, the lead singer of Alabama, actually came to our studio and performed live as a way to help the state and the region try to piece itself together. He was there for the better part of four hours and when he closed the show by singing "My Home's in Alabama," I'm not sure there was a dry eye in the studio. We weren't the only ones dabbing their eyes. We heard from friends and strangers alike who said they had sat in their cars and listened to Randy as tears rolled down their cheeks. Another person said he had listened to the entire show while driving from Mobile to Birmingham and was so moved by the performance that he needed to pull off the road to compose himself.

I'd like to believe that, thanks to Randy, we eased a tiny bit of the pain.

Saban also came on the show in the wake of the tornado tragedies. He wasn't there as the Tide football coach so much, but as an Alabaman trying to help other Alabamans. He and his wife, Terry, have helped build and support more than a dozen Habitat for Humanity homes for families devastated by those 2011 tornadoes.

A lot of people thought I was done in the business when my WJOX contract expired. At least one national media writer observed I was noticeably absent from an elaborate press conference in Atlanta when the birth of the SEC Network was officially announced in early May 2013

(ESPN executives, SEC officials and thirty-one SEC coaches were in attendance, but no Finebaum). That only fueled the rumors that I was finished.

The rumors were wrong. A few weeks later, on May 21, Rachel Bachman broke the story in the *Wall Street Journal* of my return, under the headline, "Finebaum Ends His Silence."

My stay on Elba lasted about six months. I was hired by ESPN in late May, made my first official ESPN appearance at the SEC Football Media Days in July and my radio show returned to the air on August 11.

Generally speaking, I'd rather be trapped in an elevator with Dee Snider than attend the SEC Media Days. Anybody with a heartbeat can cover the event. I'm not sure there are fifty legitimate members of the media covering the Media Days. But it has become a tradition and there's no turning back.

I'll give the SEC credit for creating something out of nothing. The Media Days are the equivalent of a three-day press conference. It is mind-numbingly dull during most years. After all, there are only so many times you can hear a coach go through his team's two-deep roster.

The event is held in suburban Birmingham, in a hotel that is attached to a shopping mall. Fans (most of them Tide fans) pour into the lobby hoping to catch a glimpse of a player or coach.

They go nuts when they see Saban. It is like Elvis has returned to the building, or Michael Jackson is in the house because he forgot a white glove. Cameras flash. People scream. Sharpies and 8x10 photos are offered for autographs.

Saban will wade into the crowd for a few minutes. He doesn't have to; he could sneak in and out the back way. I'll give him his due: he doesn't take the fans for granted.

It isn't just a Saban thing, though. The Bama fans used to go nuts when they saw Mike Shula. At least now, they have a reason to go nuts. Saban has won actual games and championships.

Tim Tebow was always a headliner at the SEC Media Days. Spurrier could draw a crowd. Then–Tennessee coach Phillip Fulmer could draw a subpoena (he was served with one during the 2008 Media Days).

I've always thought the SEC ought to sell tickets to the Media Days and take it on the road. Make it like the annual Cubs Convention in Chicago. Fans would love it.

Take it to Atlanta, Nashville, Orlando, New Orleans. Let the fans ask the same dumb, formulaic questions the media asks ("Coach Saban, can you talk about [fill in the blank]"). I mean, it's not like anything important is ever said at the Media Days.

I never thought any player could surpass Tebow for sheer star power. When Tebow was at Florida, he helped push the SEC to another level of excellence and Q ratings. He transcended the sport.

Then along came Johnny Manziel.

I've covered the SEC Media Days for years, and Manziel's appearance in 2013 was the most bizarre ever. He and his persona sucked the air out of the place. Tebow who? Fulmer what? Saban where? Who cares!

The Alabama fans in attendance didn't know whether to boo him or genuflect. A season earlier he had led the Aggies to the signature upset of the season, beating seemingly invincible Bama at Bryant Denny Stadium. There are Crimson Tide followers who still can't believe it happened.

Manziel had the nickname ("Johnny Football"). He had the charisma. He had the bad boy reputation.

The 2012 Heisman Trophy winner had had your typical college player existence during the off-season. He had gone to class, worked out, spent time reading Scripture.

I'm sorry—that was Tebow. Manziel spent his off-season doing the Letterman and Leno shows, waving wads of money at an Oklahoma casino, attending the Super Bowl, Mardi Gras, the NBA Finals, throwing out the first pitch at big-league ball games, hanging with

LeBron, vacationing in Cabo, playing golf at Pebble Beach and, oh, yeah, making an unceremonious departure from the Manning Passing Academy after missing a meeting.

A year earlier, Manziel's name was barely mentioned at the SEC Media Days. He was a quarterback at Texas A&M, nothing more.

Now he was bigger than Tebow. Now he overwhelmed college football just as Tebow had.

I had voted for Manziel to win the 2012 Heisman. But his off-season schedule was the stuff of movie stars, not redshirt sophomores. I thought he was trending toward a train wreck, and now it appeared the prophecy was coming true.

Manziel walked into the place a little after 8 a.m. and everybody engulfed him. It was like Ali walking into the room. I'd never seen anything like it.

He was brought to the ESPN set, where he told Joe Tessitore that his phone had died at the Manning Academy, which is why his alarm didn't work, which is why he overslept and missed a meeting at the camp.

Had he been drinking (as was reported in some circles) at the camp? "I'm not going into details," said Manziel.

Manziel said he hadn't been expelled from the camp. He said his departure was "a mutual decision."

After the interview, ESPN asked for my take on Manziel's comments. I wasn't buying it. Something didn't add up.

His roommate wouldn't have woken him? Someone from the Manning Camp wouldn't have stopped by? His leaving was a "mutual decision"? To me, it was just the latest in a series of public missteps for Johnny Football.

Manziel would later tell reporters that he had made "mistakes" in the past and that he had learned from those mistakes. And then he said, "I guess I feel like Justin Bieber or something."

Or something.

I pulled for him in 2012. He was new, fresh and unlike any player we had seen. But I didn't find him all that likeable in July 2013. His off-season antics made me reassess—and I wasn't the only one to do so. We in the media had helped create and feed his image as Johnny Football, so there was blame to go around. But it was clear that Manziel had embraced the image. He liked the attention. He liked being the centerpiece of the 2013 season.

The questions were obvious: Could he win a second consecutive Heisman? Could he beat Alabama again? Could he stay out of trouble?

When the three days were finished, I had to admit that I'd actually enjoyed myself. Muschamp had said that Saban was in a legacy-building mode. And you couldn't help but laugh when Saban mocked the media's preseason picks, saying that if he got as many things wrong as the media did with its predictions, he'd be back in West Virginia running his father's gas station.

That wasn't very nice to say, especially after we had picked Bama to win the SEC West (followed by A&M, LSU, Ole Miss, Auburn, Mississippi State and Arkansas), as well as the SEC Championship. In the East, we had chosen Georgia, followed by South Carolina, Florida, Vanderbilt, Tennessee, Missouri and Kentucky.

South Carolina's Jadeveon Clowney, supposedly the best player in the country, had actually received the second-most votes for preseason first-team defense (behind Bama linebacker C. J. Mosley). Clowney was a Media Days blip compared to the Johnny Football hysteria. Manziel even eclipsed the appearance of Alabama quarterback (and fellow Manning Academy camper) AJ McCarron.

A few weeks later came the debut of my ESPN radio show. That first show was very awkward. I was in a new city (Charlotte) and a new studio, and I hadn't done a live show in more than six months.

It helped to hear familiar voices: Legend, Tammy, Jim from Tuscaloosa, Robert from Waterloo, Charles from Reeltown. Even

Taylor Hicks called from Las Vegas to sing a song. They missed me, and I hadn't realized how much I missed them.

The callers had helped get me here, so I wanted the first half hour of the show to be devoted entirely to them. Only then did we bring on our first guest.

As choppy as the first show was, I still loved being back. It had been a long absence, or as sportswriter Cecil Hurt put it when he appeared on the show, "It's been so long, the last time we talked, Manti Te'o's girlfriend was still real."

It was Manziel who got the show moving again. In early August, a few days before my return to radio, ESPN reported that the NCAA was investigating allegations that the A&M star had been paid to sign autographs. If the report was true, Manziel could be suspended. And depending on the length of the suspension, his absence could have huge ramifications for his team, the SEC race, the national championship race and Manziel's Heisman hopes.

In late August, Manziel was reinstated by the NCAA for an "inadvertent" rules violation related to those autograph signings. A ticket broker who had made several of the accusations had refused to cooperate with the NCAA's investigation. So there wasn't much the NCAA could do. In the end, it imposed a first-half suspension of Manziel in the August 31 season opener against Rice.

I don't know if Manziel took money for autographs. Maybe he did, maybe he didn't. It doesn't matter. He had put himself in a position where it was plausible that he'd accepted money and broken NCAA rules. He had put A&M in the position of having to squirm again at another Johnny Football off-field incident. It was a punklike thing to do.

The NCAA penalty was barely a hand slap. In fact, an actual hand slap would have been more meaningful.

You could hear the sigh of relief all the way from College Station. You could hear it from the SEC offices in Birmingham. You could hear it from the CBS offices in New York and the ESPN offices in Bristol, Connecticut.

Manziel was must-see college football. His game had brilliant moments of spontaneity and improvisation. He might have been a knucklehead kid off the field, but he was mesmerizing on it. No player confounded defensive coordinators more than Manziel.

Every player, according to Nick Saban, has tendencies. Every player, except one: Johnny Football. His only tendency is to do the unexpected. A play sent in from the sidelines is only a starting point to him. He has the freedom—and the talent—to change everything on the fly. You can't game-plan, said Saban, against a quarterback whose strategy is to have no strategy. It's maddening. It's effective.

Manziel had sat out that first half against Rice in the Aggies' season opener and then come in and thrown six completions, three of them for touchdowns. A&M had won by 21 points.

Against Sam Houston State, he threw for 426 yards and three touchdowns and ran for another.

His next opponent wouldn't be another Football Championship Subdivision (FCS) program like Sam Houston. It would be the guy who had been trying to figure him out for months.

It would be Saban.

What do the moon and A&M have in common?
We control the Tide.

—TEXAS A&M ATHLETIC DIRECTOR ERIC HYMAN TO AN
AGGIES BOOSTER CLUB IN JUNE 2013

CHAPTER 5

Aggies, Yellers and Collies

Saturday, September 14, 2013

College Station, Texas

THE SEASON SKINNY: An officiating crew brain cramp costs Wisconsin a last-second chance to beat Arizona State. . . . Duke loses its ACC opener to Georgia Tech. . . . UCF records its first-ever win against a Big Ten team with its victory at Penn State. . . . Auburn ends its ten-game SEC losing streak with a comeback win against Mississippi State.

So I'm talking the other day with my new best buddy, Texas governor Rick Perry, and he was saying—

Oh, wait, you mean you don't get calls from the governor of the state with the second-biggest economy in the country? I didn't, either—until Texas A&M joined the SEC. Since then, the governor and I have talked so much football that he might appoint me to his cabinet.

Only the SEC can bring together a U.S. presidential candidate and a sports talk show host. Not that I'm complaining.

I first met Governor Perry while I was the emcee of a 2012 scholarship dinner at Texas A&M in honor of Gene Stallings, a former Aggies head coach and A&M alum (I'm sorry—they're officially called "Former Students"). The governor is also a Former Student (Class of '72) and was one of the featured speakers at the event.

We sat next to each other during the dinner and chatted about all things SEC and A&M. It was the Aggies' first season as an SEC member and Perry was excited about the possibilities. And it was obvious that he, like every other Aggie I've ever met, thought A&M was the greatest thing since Instagram.

Later in the year, at the annual National Football Foundation Hall of Fame dinner in New York, I saw the governor again. This time he invited my wife and me to stay with him when Alabama faced A&M in College Station in 2013. I thought he was just being polite.

On August 30, 2013, my phone rang.

It was the governor. And when I say "the governor," I don't mean his administrative assistant or aide, issuing an invitation on behalf of Perry for the Bama-A&M game.

"Paul, Rick Perry here," he said.

"Governor," I said, not entirely sure this wasn't some sort of gag.

"Howdy," he said. "I want to make sure we spend some quality time together. I want you to have a full appreciation of Texas A&M."

I thought the whole thing was utterly bizarre. Didn't he have a state to run?

I've spent time around politicians. Most of them have perfected the art of acting to make it seem they're interested in you when they're actually not. They're like cotton candy—99 percent hot air, 1 percent sugar.

Governor Perry is different. I'm not saying he isn't a politician, but he had extended an invitation the previous December and now he was following up on it. How about that? A politician who keeps his promises.

So he gave me a tour of the place. I had been to College Station several times, but never with the state's governor as my tour guide. It was a gas. Governor Perry not only wanted me to see the A&M sights, but he wanted me to understand the culture of the place.

A&M has a different feel to it than any other school in the SEC—for that matter, than any other school in the country.

There's a cultish quality to the place—and I don't mean that in a bad way. When you walk around campus, people don't stare at their feet when they pass. They look you in the eye, smile and say, "Howdy."

It's not the prettiest school you'll ever see. I've been to more picturesque campuses, including the one in Austin. But I can't think of another place where the students take more pride in their college than A&M.

I'm a dog person. My wife and I have an Australian shepherd named Trooper. He's a sweetie, right up until the moment he thinks a stranger is going to do my wife and me harm. Then he's more ferocious than Tammy going after an Auburn-basher.

By the way, my wife wants to go to a football game about as often as Mississippi State plays in the SEC Championship. But in November 2012, she wanted to see Johnny Football make his debut at Bryant-Denny Stadium.

By the end of the first quarter, the Aggies led, 20–0, and Bama fans were in a panic. The last time the Tide had trailed by as many as 14 points was over two years earlier—and Bama had lost that game, against South Carolina. When A&M had taken a 7–0 lead, it was Bama's largest deficit of the 2012 season.

It was a shocking development, and it would end with a shocking result: Johnny Football 29, Bama 24.

But long before the final play, I received a text from Linda, who was sitting on the opposite side of the stadium press box. She had a question.

"Do you know the name of that cute dog on the A&M sideline?" she asked.

Actually, I did. Her name is Reveille VIII and she's the A&M mascot. She has her own Facebook page, which must mean she can type better than I can. I learned that Reveille is the highest-ranking member of the school's Corps of Cadets. I learned that the Cadets address her as "Miss Rev, ma'am," and that if she jumps onto the bed of a Cadet and falls asleep, the Cadet has to sleep on the floor rather than disturb her. I learned that if her handler (she has an entire Cadet entourage that looks out for her) is in class and Reveille barks during the professor's lesson, the class is to be dismissed immediately.

I wish Reveille had been around when I was in school—and in a barking kind of mood.

The Seattle Seahawks make a big deal about the Twelfth Man, but A&M's student body has called itself the Twelfth Man since 1922. In fact, the phrase was trademarked by the school in 1990, which explains why A&M later sued the Seahawks for claiming the Twelfth Man as their own. (Seattle ownership paid a lump sum licensing fee of $100,000, as well as a $5,000 annual fee.)

A&M is the only place, as my *GameDay* colleague Tom Rinaldi once observed, where they practice yelling. That's right—one of the coolest things you'll ever see is Yell Practice, held in front of a packed house at Kyle Field the night before a home game.

A&M has the largest military marching band in the country. Here in the South, we respect the military. The precision marching of the Fightin' Texas Aggie Band, comprised entirely of Corps of Cadets members, is the exact opposite of the floppy hat anarchy of Stanford's band.

A&M has yell leaders, and "Gig 'Em" signs, and military memorials (please don't step on the grass outside the Memorial Student Center). It has character and characters, including one Johnny Manziel. It has tradition, history and money. Lots of money.

The Aggies were meant for the SEC like clams were meant for chowder. I talked to former Aggies coach R. C. Slocum about it. Slocum, the winningest head coach in A&M football history and now a special adviser to the school's president, said Texas A&M considered a move to the SEC in mid-1990s, but then-Governor Ann Richards short-circuited the deal.

There were critics of the move back then, but you can't find them now. Slocum said the SEC is the perfect fit geographically, philosophically and time zone–wise.

"I don't know of any reason why it would have been bad for us to move," Slocum said. "But still, it was a really bold decision. We said,

'Let's just look and see what's best for A&M. We can decide what's best for us. We've been around a hundred years.' "

Some Aggies still fret over giving the SEC entry into the state's rich recruiting areas. But SEC programs have been cherry-picking recruits in Texas for years. And how about the flip side: A&M now gains entry to SEC recruiting strongholds.

This is a win-win-win. A win for the SEC. A win for A&M. A win for me, thanks to my pal, the gov.

We've brought our radio show to A&M for the Bama game. And *GameDay* is on-site too. I see T-shirts in the campus bookstore that read, "Heisman Football," in tribute to Manziel, who is going for the Heisman Trophy repeat. Some of our callers aren't as respectful of Johnny Football. They don't like his penchant for publicity, for off-season silliness and for his involvement, at whatever level, in the auto-graph sessions that resulted in the NCAA's suspending Manziel for the first half of A&M's season opener.

"He's so in love with hisself," said one caller. "I just despise him!"

I'm not so crazy about him, either. A great player is becoming a punch line—and it is his own fault. Beginning with his "I'm-the-victim" Tweets, his disrespectful antics at the Manning Passing Academy, his brain-dead decision to do autograph sessions (the NCAA is dumb, but not that dumb, Johnny), his on-field scoreboard pointing and money-squeeze gestures, his unsportsmanlike conduct penalties. He had said it himself at the SEC Media Days: he was the Biebs of college football. But everybody was talking about him for all the wrong reasons. It was compelling theater, but there was an element of sadness to it.

Think about this: Manziel's own teammates didn't vote him as one of the Aggies' captains. The returning Heisman winner isn't even a team captain?

It isn't a coincidence that a high-profile college coach told ESPN. com that if he were coaching Manziel, "I would kick his ass." An-other coach of a program in the top twenty-five said: "Someone needs to step on [Manziel's] neck. He must be killing the locker room . . . and he's killing the program for the next two, three years. Why isn't anyone stopping him? Is the kid screaming out for help? He's costing himself money in the [NFL] draft. I would tell Dad to take him and his kid back home."

To cap it all off, I had also been critical of Texas A&M chancellor John Sharp. Sharp had wrongly criticized ESPN's reporting of the Manziel autograph controversy and had added that Manziel was innocent of any wrongdoing connected to the autograph sessions.

I had compared Sharp with one of the laughingstocks of our era, former Vanderbilt chancellor/Brown president/Ohio State president Gordon Gee. Gee is a bow-tied clown who was forced to resign at Ohio State earlier in 2013 after making anti-Catholic remarks during the 2012 season. Gee had also taken shots at the playing schedules of teams such as Boise State and the academic commitment of the SEC.

Gee always plays to his audience. He is the king of the cheap laugh.

I do the same thing sometimes. But I'm a radio host, not the chancellor or president of a university. It would have been one thing had Gee's anti–Notre Dame/Catholic comments been an isolated incident. But Gee has a long history of insulting people, places and things. I've always wondered if his signature bow tie is tied so tight that it cuts off the circulation to his brain.

I don't normally call for someone's dismissal just because they push the envelope in their public comments. Using that standard, I'd be out of a job. But in Gee's case, enough was enough. It was time for Ohio State to drop-kick him out of his office.

So when A&M's Sharp had taken a shot at what I thought was thorough reporting on ESPN's part, I said I was glad we had identified "the next Gordon Gee."

With our show making an appearance in College Station, it was a good time to have Sharp as a guest on the program. I was a little apprehensive about the situation. After all, there has been some trash-talking going on between the two parties.

As the Friday afternoon interview began, it became apparent that Sharp had forgotten or had chosen to ignore my criticisms of him. Instead, he talked about the Aggie spirit, about how the school was always going to come to the defense of one of its own—in this case, Manziel.

"I just happened to know that Johnny was not wrong," Sharp said.

Really? Never mind that the NCAA thought Manziel had done wrong, which is why he got the wrist slap half-game suspension. But I was going to let the chancellor have his say. And he certainly did.

He said he had gotten to know Manziel while spending time with him at Boy Scout banquets and state legislature appearances.

"My momma wishes I was as good as a kid as Johnny Manziel," he said.

Out of fairness, I reminded the chancellor that I had compared him with Gee.

"Oh, I remember now," he said. "Gee is a good friend of mine. He called me and told me about that."

Then I asked him about A&M's leaving the Big 12 and breaking free of the magnetic force field that had been the University of Texas.

"We don't have any schools in our windshield anymore," he said proudly. "They're behind us now."

He's right. the Aggies finished 11-2 in 2012 and entered the 2013 season with the most dynamic and recognizable player in all of football. They had crushed former Big 12 partner Oklahoma in the Cotton Bowl and had upset No. 1 Alabama earlier in the 2012 regular season. They also had one of the most interesting coaches in the business. Sumlin is bright and charismatic. He's one of the few coaches that you actually *want* to talk to. You can have a conversation with him, which is a lot different from having an interview.

Meanwhile, Texas was coming off a 9-4 (5-4 in conference play) season in 2012 and Mack Brown was feeling the heat. And that was before the Longhorns had lost their second game of the 2013 season to BYU, giving up 550 rushing yards during the embarrassing defeat. And did I mention that A&M routinely outrecruits Texas these days?

The folks at A&M bought into the SEC move from Day One like A&M people buy into everything: boots first, in a bigger-than-Texas, Nestea-plunge way. And I love that about A&M people. Once they make up their minds about something, they're all in. There's no equivocating, no waffling.

A&M reminded me of Florida's program twenty years ago—if it ever figured things out, it would be tough to contain. Well, A&M has finally figured it out, thanks to the move to the SEC.

Bear Bryant coached at A&M and eventually ended up at Bama. He used to walk around College Station as a kid. Stallings coached at A&M and eventually ended up Bama. Even before it joined the SEC, one of A&M's most frequent nonconference rivals was LSU. So the Aggies weren't entirely unfamiliar with their new home.

I'm intrigued by Texas A&M. I see greatness-to-be. For so many years A&M was the stepchild to Texas, much like Auburn has been to Alabama. But I don't see that anymore. The shroud has been lifted and A&M is out of the Big 12, and out of Texas's burnt orange shadow. I think the Aggies will be a force in the SEC and college football for a very long time.

First of all, A&M has a formidable fan base. When those people unite behind something or someone, watch out. They can move the needle. Or let me put it this way: of all the programs in the SEC, I think A&M poses the greatest long-term threat to Alabama's dominance. Greater than Auburn, than LSU, than Florida.

A&M's recruiting base is massive. A&M's facilities and stadium are expanding. A&M's resources are unmatched. There's a buzz to the program. No wonder Sumlin hasn't left the place.

As they prepare to play No. 1 Bama, the Aggies are feeling pretty good about themselves, and with good reason.

They have history (a win at Tuscaloosa in 2012, for starters) and Johnny Football on their side. If Manziel can beat the Tide for a second consecutive year, it won't matter what he did during the off-season.

Just before I make my Saturday morning *GameDay* appearance, I see someone at the back of the crowd waving a poster with a photo of me on it. I have a fan!

I squint to better see the sign. Yes, it is me all right. Dressed as a clown.

Security personnel remove the sign and place it on a pile of other offending signs, though I don't know why. It is a funny sign. Someone has put some effort into it. When you do what I do for a living, you expect those sorts of things. In honor of the fallen poster, I take a photo of it and make it my Twitter avatar.

After the show, George Whitfield, the quarterback guru who works with Manziel and is now a contributor to *GameDay*, wants to know if I'd like to meet Paul Manziel, Johnny's father.

George introduces us and then leaves the room. Paul and I talk for about twenty minutes, and never once does he bring up my past criticisms of his son.

Paul acknowledges that Johnny had some off-field issues that need to be addressed—and says that they will be addressed. Johnny, he adds, is dealing with the growing pains of celebrity.

He tells me about how Johnny had originally wanted to go to Oregon, but had changed his mind. He says he knew early on that Johnny was destined for athletic greatness.

If you close your eyes, you would think you were listening to Earl Woods talk about his prodigy, Tiger. Paul Manziel believes in his son, to the point where I wondered if he believes in him too much.

I respect his devotion to his son. But I still worry that Johnny has the potential to self-destruct.

The game against Alabama is going to help determine his legacy. If he plays poorly and A&M loses, people will simply move on to the next circus. If he plays well and the Aggies pull off another upset of top-ranked Bama, he will achieve demigod status. If it happens, you can engrave his name again on the Heisman Trophy. Not in December, but in September.

As it turns out, A&M loses, 49–42, but Manziel still throws for 464 yards and five touchdowns, rushes for 98 yards and causes Saban to age before our eyes. If Manziel declares early for the NFL Draft, nobody is going to be happier to see him leave than Saban. The Bama coach can't figure out how to stop the guy.

Manziel does throw two killer interceptions in the game, one of which is returned for a 73-yard touchdown, marring an otherwise spectacular effort.

Manziel has the highlights, but AJ McCarron has another W. The "game manager" is all grown up, throwing for 334 yards, four touchdowns and completing 20 of 29 passes.

Despite the victory, there are some warning signs that this isn't the same Bama juggernaut of 2012. Saban teams don't give up 42 points. This is the first time since he was hired at Bama in 2007 that a Saban-coached team has given up this many points.

I'm like everybody else. I figure it is Manziel-related, nothing more. I figure wrong.

It's been twelve, thirteen, fourteen years now I've been listening to him. It's kind of like the *Sgt. Pepper's* Beatles cover. You keep seeing things, noticing things.

—I-MAN

Roll Call

Saturday, September 21, 2013
Birmingham, Alabama

THE SEASON SKINNY: Danny Sheridan releases his early BCS Championship odds: Bama 2/1, Oregon 3/1, Ohio state 10/1, UGA and Louisville 12/1, Clemson and FSU 15/1. . . . Heisman voter Todd McShay of ESPN says he holds Johnny Football in higher regard than before the Bama loss. . . . Saban tells reporters asking about the rumors of him going to Texas, "Quite frankly, I'm just too damn old to start over somewhere else." . . . I'm bored: only one game featuring two ranked teams, Arizona State vs. Stanford.

f I were ranking the programs in the SEC with the best overall football curb appeal (a martini mix of tradition, facilities, media exposure, recruiting, ability to win consistently, coaching, stability and the IT Factor), it would go like this:

1. ALABAMA

2. FLORIDA

3. LSU

4. GEORGIA

5. TENNESSEE

6. TEXAS A&M

7. AUBURN

8. SOUTH CAROLINA

9. ARKANSAS

10. OLE MISS

11. MISSISSIPPI STATE

12. MISSOURI

13. VANDERBILT

14. KENTUCKY

Alabama is the Amazon of the SEC. But what happens when Bama loses its Jeff Bezos? One of these days Saban isn't going to be on the Bama sideline. Then what?

Athletic director Bill Battle has been planning for that day. Or at least he had better be planning for it. In the top drawer of his desk there should be a wish list of five candidates to replace Saban. It should be updated constantly. And when the time comes, it should include the input of Saban, who could be an invaluable resource.

I used to think Bama defensive coordinator Kirby Smart would be his successor. Smart is making a million-plus in salary and has turned down opportunities to coach elsewhere—probably because he thought he had a good chance to succeed Saban. But now I'm not sure if he's the front-runner. Whoever gets the job isn't likely to win at the same level as Saban has. But there's no way Bama will return to the depressing DuBose/Shula days, either. Thank the man in the Panama hat for that. The foundation is too strong for Bama not to remain a top-flight program, with or without Saban.

Florida, by comparison, is Samsung. It has the smart and pragmatic Jeremy Foley, who is the best athletic director in the nation. It has the infrastructure and the recruiting base to succeed. And it has the next Saban: Will Muschamp. Of all the young coaches in the SEC—and because of all the built-in advantages of a program such as Florida's (facilities, recruiting base, weather, quality of the school)—he has the most potential for success. Unfortunately, Florida also has one of the most insufferable fan bases. There's a great line from the legendary sportswriter Dan Jenkins. He said that Florida people had "the arrogance of Alabama and the record of Wake Forest."

For so many years, Florida fans were arrogant for no logical reason. It's not like the Gators were winning conference or national championships.

Then in 1979 along came Charley Pell, who turned the program into a rising power. Florida followers probably don't want me to mention that Pell also committed about ten thousand NCAA violations and was fired during the 1984 season, or that Florida's championship SEC results of that year were vacated.

Spurrier returned to his alma mater in 1990 and gave Florida a swagger. His timing was perfect: the league was going through a transition (Alabama and LSU were up and down, Pat Dye was in his final seasons at Auburn), nobody could stop his innovative Fun 'N Gun offense, and his visor throws and sharp-tongued barbs translated perfectly to television. He defied Dan Jenkins and made Florida football into the Florida football it is today. Urban Meyer moved the chains, and we'll see what Muschamp does over time. But the standard has been set. Gators followers expect nothing less than championships. So does Foley.

I've had people in the business tell me that coaching LSU is *the* best job in the country. Because there's no real in-state competition, you have the pick of all of Louisiana's great high school players (and there are lots of them). And if you've never been to a night game at LSU, I'll tell you what it's like: three hours of decibel hell. The place is so loud they should call it Deaf Valley. Just don't trip over the empty bourbon bottles.

Georgia has everything you want in a program. It is LSU without the Cajun.

Tennessee is still living in the past, but it has tradition, championships, Neyland Stadium, a new football facility, the world's most annoying fight song and, at last, a strategy for the future. Unlike the Derek Dooley of yore, who always coached like he was making it up as he went along, Butch Jones has a football plan, his so-called brick-by-brick philosophy, which sounds corny but actually might work. He has filtered out some of the toxicity and drama in the locker room. He has reached out to former Vols stars for support and advice. He has recruited as if his job depends on it, which it does. Dooley could rarely close the deal.

Tennessee is on its fourth head coach since 2008, so it would be nice if it got this one right. Maybe if it does, it might stand a chance of landing the next Peyton Manning. Jones has already landed his signature. In his office is an autographed Tennessee helmet. Manning wrote on it, "Coach Jones, I'm in your corner."

Texas A&M could rule this conference within five years, maybe less. I'm a huge fan of Sumlin. If Sumlin stays in College Station, there's no stopping the Aggies.

Auburn lives in Alabama's houndstooth shadow, but it has pride, resources and now Malzahn, who understands the culture of the place (he was the offensive coordinator when the Tigers won the national championship in 2010) and knows how to score points.

As long as Spurrier remains at South Carolina, Clemson will weep and Georgia and Florida won't rest easy.

The Razorbacks will be relevant again. But I love that former SEC-basher Bielema is the guy in charge of the turnaround.

Ole Miss has run out of Mannings to recruit. It had Archie. It had Cooper. It had Eli. But I predict a program breakthrough if Hugh Freeze keeps winning the battle of the ballcaps on National Signing Day. The Rebels had some momentum under Tommy Tuberville, had it for a moment under David Cutcliffe, lost it completely under Ed Orgeron, got it back briefly under Houston Nutt and then lost it again. For some reason, Ole Miss can't seem to sustain any success.

Coaching Mississippi State is the toughest job in the SEC. In a state where there isn't a huge recruiting base, Dan Mullen has to compete against Ole Miss and Southern Miss for players. The University of Saban is about ninety minutes away. LSU overshadows the Bulldogs' program in the southern part of the state. And Nobel laureate William Faulkner didn't live in Starkville; he lived in stately Oxford, home of Ole Miss.

Mississippi State has no advantages over its rivals, unless you count cowbells. But when they get it right every so often, it's also one of the toughest places to win a game as a visiting team.

I've got a tiny soft spot for Mississippi State. I just feel bad for its football program.

I used to think having Mullen as the Bulldogs' head coach was an advantage, but now I'm not so sure. I considered him a can't-miss prospect—and then he sort of missed.

Missouri is a dark-horse program. It's not Texas A&M, but in the long run, Mizzou is going to carry its SEC weight.

When it joined the league in 2012, Missouri was a tough sell to me. I wasn't sure the SEC should add a team whose biggest football rival was Kansas. In the SEC, we wouldn't bother flossing our teeth with that rivalry.

But I have been impressed by how excited and doe-eyed the Missouri people were about the move from the Big 12 to the SEC. I'm not sure "appreciative" is the right word, but they were eager to be immersed into the ways of the SEC. I became their Yoda.

Tigers fans would call the show and ask for a scouting report on the league. They wanted to know what it would be like to play in this conference. And here's what I told them: It's like nothing you've ever experienced. It's like your hair is on fire. It's like Nicki Minaj is pounding on your door and she wants to go partying. Now! It's like picking a fight with Anderson Silva.

Missouri's first year in the league reminded me of the time I took my wife for her first-ever visit to New York. We were walking down Fifth Avenue and she couldn't quit pointing up at the skyscrapers, her mouth open in wonderment. They don't have buildings like that in Birmingham.

Well, they don't have the SEC in the Big 12.

Mizzou will be better equipped in 2013. Gary Pinkel is their coach and he did a nice enough job coaching the Tigers in the Big 12. But as I've told their fans, if he's going to compete in the SEC, he had better step it up.

For years—decades—I said Vandy belonged in another conference.

Vandy was the falsetto tenor in the SEC, while almost everyone else in the league was a baritone or bass.

Before James Franklin started coaching at Vandy in 2011, the Commodores had played in four bowl games since 1890.

Even with Franklin, they've never won an SEC championship or an SEC East division title. Their highest-ever SEC finish (second) came way back in 1935.

Unless Florida, Georgia and South Carolina secede from the SEC East, Vandy is never going to win the division. But at least Franklin has made it interesting.

Basketball has helped. Baseball has helped. But for the most part, I think Vandy is living off the strength of its library.

As an aside, I'm always amused by Pac-12 fans who lecture me about the greatness and grandness of Stanford football. They love telling me about the Cardinal football success story and how, if Vandy is willing to work very, very hard, it can be a stripped-down, decidedly inferior version of the great and grand Stanford football program. But only if the Commodores work very hard at it.

Yes, well, I'd like to remind Pac-12 fans that Vandy has won the exact same number of AP or UPI football national championships as the Cardinal: zero. I'd also like to remind them that Stanford doesn't play in the same conference as Alabama, Auburn, Georgia, Florida, LSU and Texas A&M. If it did, Cardinal football wouldn't be so great and grand.

I think Vanderbilt would be a perfect program for the ACC. I would boot Vandy and Kentucky out of the league and replace them with Clemson and Virginia Tech. Those are better fits.

Franklin will keep the Commodores competitive. But I'm surprised a larger program hasn't money-whipped him away from Nashville. When you do what he's done, and done it at a program such as Vandy, you're usually wooed away by one of the big-boy schools. Good for him for sticking around. But no way is he a Vandy lifer. Nobody is.

I honestly don't know what to say about Kentucky football. Sometimes I have to remind myself UK is still in the conference. I think it'd win just as many games if it let John Calipari coach both the basketball *and* football programs.

Kentucky is not a legitimate SEC football school. It cares, but it doesn't care enough to give the program anywhere near the same love it gives basketball. Seven years of Rich Brooks in the 2000s (the Wildcats played in four straight bowl games under Brooks) might be as good as it ever gets.

In a way, Kentucky football is Auburn Lite. Every so often the Wildcats will jump-start the program and then do something dumb: they lose a coach, they get in trouble, they lose momentum and can't figure out a way to recover it. Maybe Mark Stoops will be the exception, but he has some huge obstacles facing him, not least among them that the fan base there becomes instantly uninterested once basketball practice begins. But I did see one small sign of hope: Kentucky's 2013 spring game drew more than 50,000 people. And recruiting has improved under Stoops. Then again, it couldn't have gotten worse.

Nothing against Stoops—he could end up being the savior of that program—but I would have hired Bobby Petrino. If you're a top player in the state of Kentucky, there has to be a compelling reason to keep you from going to rival Louisville or going out of state. Love him or hate him, Petrino might have been that reason.

There's a reason why Louisville's football program has lapped Kentucky's: U of L athletic director Tom Jurich's willingness to take chances and hire strong-willed, charismatic coaches. He hired Petrino as head coach in late 2002. He hired Charlie Strong in 2010. In basketball, he hired Rick Pitino in 2001.

Petrino was a great hire, if you can ignore ten years of idiocy. In 2003, less than a year after getting the Louisville job, he had what he thought was a secret meeting with Auburn administrators, only to read about it in the papers the next day. In 2004, he kicked the tires on the soon-to-be-available Florida job and later met with LSU officials about possibly succeeding Saban, who had left for the Miami Dolphins. In 2006, he interviewed with the Oakland Raiders. Then he signed a ten-year deal with U of L, vowing that "Louisville is my home."

Less than six months later he left "home" to become the head coach of the Atlanta Falcons, where he stayed for a matter of months before instructing a staff member to leave a lovely seventy-eight-word I'm-outta-here form letter in each Falcons player's locker.

Arkansas didn't care. Petrino won games and brought the Hogs back into the national football consciousness.

And then on April 1, 2012—Petrino Fool's Day—he crashed his motorcycle on a rural Arkansas road.

His twenty-five-year-old mistress, a former Arkansas volleyball player who had gotten her job in the athletic department because of Petrino's patronage, was on the back of the motorcycle. Petrino, who suffered four broken ribs and a cracked vertebra in the crash, tried to cover up that messy fact by deliberately misleading Arkansas athletic director Jeff Long about the details of the accident and his relationship with Jessica Dorrell. He did the same thing during his first news conference after the accident. Petrino, married and a father of four, lied until he could lie no more. The public release of the accident report exposed the cover-up.

For the next two weeks the Petrino scandal dominated the spring chatter of SEC football. Everybody was drawn to the wreckage of Petrino's life. The scandal had every important ingredient: sex, a secret affair, a coach of a team expected to make a run at the national championship, a crash, a cover-up, a firing, followed by the emergency hiring of a goofball (John L. Smith). Am I missing anything?

We had sex therapists on the show to discuss the broader topic of infidelity. We had marriage counselors. Preachers. I thought I was stuck in a Dr. Phil parallel universe.

Finally, Petrino himself came on the show. I had met with him

92

before, during his hiatus, when he was on the mend. At the time, he needed all the friends he could get.

He made a good argument, offered all the requisite mea culpas. I talked to him for about an hour or so. He wanted back into coaching.

We talked with him when he got the job at Western Kentucky in December 2012. He wasn't a great interview, but by then he had been coached up and had memorized his responses.

There are people who say Petrino has no ethics, no morals. They first point to his 2003 clandestine meeting with Auburn. Granted, the circumstances were dodgy, borderline sleazy, but I don't blame him for listening to the pitch. Lots of coaches would have done the same. That doesn't make Petrino Man of the Year, but it doesn't make him Son of Satan, either.

Kentucky should have hired him after they got rid of Joker Phillips following the 2012 season. You can also make the argument that Auburn should have hired him after they got rid of Chizik.

Petrino had paid his dues. He'd been humiliated publicly, but had said and done all the right things in the aftermath of the scandal. He had reconciled with his wife. He had handled his rehab tour about as well as you could. It was textbook stuff.

But Auburn wasn't interested. They interviewed him for fifteen minutes on the phone. That was it. No face-to-face interview.

Kentucky should have taken the flier on Petrino. But like Auburn, it was too nervous, too concerned about how it would have played nationally.

Well, here's how it would have played: Kentucky or Auburn would have gotten bashed for a few days and then something else would have happened in the sports world and we would have all moved on. It would have been a story for a day or two, tops. And a program in need would have had a great coach.

Instead, Western Kentucky threw him a lifeline and got him on the cheap for 2013.

I'm not ignoring what Petrino did to his family and to Arkansas. What he did was stupid. But he's the one who's had to pay the price. He lost his job, his money, his reputation and, almost, his marriage. It's not like he's a minister, a doctor, or a nuclear physicist. He's just a football coach. And he knows how to win football games. Winning and losing matters. A lot. That's why Western Kentucky hired him in 2013. You think they hired him because it was the Christian thing to do? No, they want to win football games. And they get to rent Petrino for a season or two at a discounted price, before he leaves for a big-time program.

If I had a son, I'd have no problem with him playing for Petrino. Wouldn't bother me at all. He's not an ax murderer, is he?

Petrino isn't the first coach to have an affair and survive. Pitino had one and has since rebuilt his reputation and won a national championship. If he can do it, why can't Petrino?

I like Bobby. He was the only guy, other than Les Miles and Urban Meyer, who looked like he could ride on the same New Year's Day parade float as Saban. He couldn't beat him—nobody can on a regular basis—but Petrino had the bona fides to make Saban relieved he's out of the league. For now.

I ain't got nothing bad to say about Paul Finebaum. But he knows how to keep the pot stirred.

—DARRIEL FROM COLUMBUS

CHAPTER 7

I Don't Want to Name-Drop, but It Was Like Drake Was Saying to Me the Other Day . . .

Saturday, September 28
Athens, Georgia

THE SEASON SKINNY: The NCAA reduces Penn State's scholarship sanctions. . . . Florida State trails Boston College, but recovers for the win. . . . Some things never change: Florida beats Kentucky for the twenty-seventh consecutive time. . . . South Carolina defeats UCF, but loses quarterback Connor Shaw with a shoulder injury. . . . Georgia's BCS dreams still live after the win against LSU–the Bulldogs' third top-ten opponent in four games.

They love me in Georgia—the love that binds children to Brussels sprouts, Dabo Swinney to the Head Ball Coach, and Tennessee to Lane Kiffin. Athens is one of my favorite campuses, but I'm no favorite of the University of Georgia's football program. And it turns out I'm not exactly one of Drake's favorites, either.

Everyone knows Drake, the world-famous rapper, actor and sports fan. And now Drake knows who I am.

Drake and Johnny Manziel are buddies—you know, just like a lot of Texas A&M students are buddies with international recording stars. Drake was on *SportsCenter* earlier this week and the subject turned to his friendship with Manziel and the criticism the Aggies quarterback had received for his on- and off-field antics and decisions.

"At the end of the day he's a great guy," said Drake to *SportsCenter* anchor Jay Crawford. "He's got the best intentions. He does nothing with malicious intent. I love him to death."

Then Crawford played a July 17 clip of me ripping Manziel at the SEC Media Days, where I sarcastically asked if Johnny Football would go to London "and await the royal birth at Buckingham Palace. What else can this young man do?"

Then they cut to me live, where Drake compared me to a history teacher he used to have in school. "He's already too stern," said Drake.

How do you debate Drake? You don't.

"This is where the middle-aged, bald guy waves the white flag," I said, waving a pocket square in surrender.

Drake was no dummy. He acknowledged that a certain level of discipline was expected of Manziel. "But I also think that people assume and read into his personal decisions a little too much . . . I will stand by the fact that he is a pure soul. . . . He's not a wild guy."

OK, I'll have to take Drake's word for it.

Meanwhile, I had to deal with Georgia fans in Athens. If only they were as polite and good-natured as Drake had been.

The Bulldogs and I have always had a love-hate relationship. If my rental car ever gets a flat in Athens, I'll expect UGA fans to stop and puncture the other three tires.

That's OK; they're not the first ones to hold a grudge. And I don't take it personally, though I still need to know who to bill for my ruined coat and shirt of 2008. (More on that later.)

I have been hard on Georgia coach Mark Richt through the years. He has been at UGA since 2001 and has a combined total of zero national championship appearances to show for it. He's won three SEC Championships, and the highest one of his teams has ever finished in the AP poll is No. 2 in 2007. His 2008 team was the AP preseason No. 1, but finished thirteenth at season's end. During his tenure, Florida, LSU, Alabama and Auburn have won national championships, but not Georgia.

How 'bout them Dawgs!

It's not like Richt has coached a bunch of mopes. I'll give you just the short list of the star players he's had: Jon Stinchcomb, David Pollack, David Greene, Thomas Davis, Knowshon Moreno, A. J. Green, Matthew Stafford, Geno Atkins, Jarvis Jones, Ben Jones, Aaron Murray and Todd Gurley.

Richt is guilty of being too loyal to his assistant coaches (he waited way too long before he dismissed guys such as Willie Martinez and Jon Jancek), not securing the recruiting borders of his state (too many great Georgia high school players are on other SEC rosters), not recruiting well on the offensive line and not paying enough attention to detail, especially when it comes to special teams.

And despite all of that, he's the best coach never to have won a national championship. Plus, I genuinely like him as a person. He's real, cares about his players (sometimes to a fault—see his reaction after the 2012 SEC Championship, when someone asked him a clumsily worded question about Murray not being able to win big games) and has overcome personal and family issues with a rare dignity. He's as decent a man as you'll ever meet.

Given where he is and the talent level of the players he's coached, should he have won more games and titles? Absolutely. But my days of bashing Richt are officially done. If he's good enough for most of the Georgia faithful, then he's good enough for me.

To be fair, Richt coaches in the meanest, baddest conference in the country. Put him in the ACC, Big Ten, Big 12, etc., and his win total would jump like LeBron.

In the SEC, he's had to coach against the best and the brightest: Spurrier (at Florida and South Carolina), Saban (at LSU and Bama), Les Miles, Phillip Fulmer, Lou Holtz, Tommy Tuberville, Bobby Petrino, James Franklin and Gus Malzahn, to name a few. And since he's been at Georgia, SEC teams have won those seven national championships.

In addition, Richt has been cursed by three plays that have cost him a chance to coach in a national title game:

Play No. 1—2002: Ohio State's Craig Krenzel completed a 37-yard pass to Michael Jenkins on fourth down to lead OSU to a 10–6 win at Purdue on November 9, 2002. If the Buckeyes had lost, Georgia probably would have played Miami for the national championship.

Play No. 2—2007: Georgia was every bit as good as the two-loss LSU team that played Ohio State for a national championship. Georgia lost to South Carolina, 16–12, and was blown out at Tennessee. UGA finished No. 2 in the country after blowing out Hawaii in the Sugar Bowl.

Play No. 3—2012: The tipped pass against Bama at the end of the SEC Championship game. If the tipped ball had fallen incomplete instead of into receiver Chris Conley's hands, Georgia would have gotten one more chance at the end zone against the Tide. If Georgia had scored (and the Tide was on its heels), the Bulldogs, not Bama, would have played Notre Dame in the BCS Championship. And we all know how that would have ended: with a crystal football trophy displayed prominently in the lobby of UGA's athletic facility.

Now Georgia faces another pivotal early-season game, this time against No. 6–ranked LSU. The Bulldogs lost at Clemson in the season opener, but have won their last two, against South Carolina and North Texas.

On Friday night I had appeared on an ESPN preview show and repeated some news that had been reported by ESPN.com's Mark Schlabach—that at the end of spring practice in 2010, Murray had contacted other coaches about a possible transfer because he thought then–UGA teammate Zach Mettenberger might win the quarterback competition. As usual, Schlabach had done his reporting. Georgia tight end Arthur Lynch, a close friend and roommate of Murray's, had been the on-the-record source for that particular news nugget.

Then this morning, as I'm walking to the *GameDay* bus not long before my first hit on the show, I hear someone yelling at me.

"Hey, Finebaum!" says the voice. "I'm Aaron Murray's uncle!"

I turn around. The man has a beer can (at 9 a.m.–ish!) and he is chasing after me.

I don't know if he's Murray's uncle or not. For Aaron's sake, I hope he isn't. But I'm not going to hang around to find out.

I make it onto the bus before the guy decides to throw the beer can at me. Lounging in the back of the bus are our two guest pickers for the show, Masters champion Bubba Watson, who played at Georgia, and LSU fan Willie Robertson of *Duck Dynasty* fame. I wonder if they're ever stalked by crazy uncles.

Just to be on the safe side, *GameDay* staffers have assigned a security guard to me for when I leave the bus. In fact, I might have two. It doesn't matter—the uncle and his beer can are gone.

This is actually the five-year anniversary, almost to the day, of my most memorable visit to Athens. The last time I was here—No. 8 Alabama vs. No. 3 Georgia in 2008—a UGA frat rat poured a beer over my head during the middle of a live shot I was doing for a Birmingham television station. (What is it about me, UGA fans and beer?)

There wasn't much I could do. I finished the TV hit and the sport coat was put to sleep. I wish the kid at least would have poured a better beer on me—it smelled like cheap Keystone. And if the fraternity had any sense of honor, it would have reimbursed me for the sport coat. Or at least taught me its secret handshake.

When it comes time for my first *GameDay* hit, the UGA crowd greets me with a heartfelt collection of boos. It touches my heart.

Chris Fowler hears the boos and jokingly mentions how popular I am with the Bulldog fans, at which point I turn to the crowd and thank it. (By the way, I pick LSU to beat Georgia.)

The topic turns to Kiffin, whose 3-1 USC team has already lost at home to Washington State and has barely beaten Utah State at the Coliseum. Kiffin is in trouble with his athletic director, with USC fans and, according to the rumors, with his own team.

When Chris asks me about the quality of the quarterback play at

USC, I quickly segue into a rant on Kiffin. How, I ask, has Kiffin gotten the head coaching jobs at the Oakland Raiders, at Tennessee and now at USC? "In some respects," I say, "Lane Kiffin is the Miley Cyrus of college football. He has very little talent, but we simply can't take our eyes off him."

On the way back to the airport, I receive some text messages from friends who know Kiffin. I ask for Kiffin's number and text him.

On Sunday morning I wake up and have six messages from the *SportsCenter* producers in Bristol. Something must have happened, but what?

Little do I know that in the wee hours of Sunday morning, Kiffin had been fired. The Trojans had lost at Arizona State, 62–41, and when the USC team plane landed in Los Angeles, Kiffin was unceremoniously dismissed by athletic director Pat Haden.

Given that USC is now 0-2 in the Pac-12 and that some USC heavy hitters were looking for any excuse to get rid of Kiffin, his firing isn't a total shock. But I do feel some level of responsibility for fanning the flames. In fact, I wish I could take a TV mulligan.

There is truth in what I said about Kiffin, but I crossed the line. By invoking the Miley Cyrus comparison, I made a much bigger splash than I had intended. In retrospect, it was unfair to Kiffin.

But from that mistake comes . . . a friendship?

It's the fire in me. It's anger. That's why I call. Back in the '90s, Paul would taunt Coach Stallings. I was in the kitchen one time and I asked my husband, "Who is that?" He said, "It's someone named Paul Finebaum." And I called him. I chewed him up and spit him out; that's what I did. Chewed him up and spit him out.

—PHYLLIS FROM MULGA

CHAPTER **8**

Radio Is a Sound Salvation.
Radio Is Cleaning Up the Nation.

Thursday, October 3, 2013
Charlotte, North Carolina

THE SEASON SKINNY: Iowa State coach Paul Rhoads has a postgame mini-meltdown after Texas stages a last minute comeback thanks to a few questionable calls by the officials. . . . Going into the Saturday games, your AP poll top five: Alabama, Oregon, Clemson, Ohio State and Stanford. Notable no-shows in the top 25: Notre Dame, Wisconsin, Auburn, UCF, Missouri and Michigan State.

I f you had ranked the top ten thousand sports talk radio show hosts in 1984, I'd have probably been on the bubble. My radio debut (*Fussin' With Finebaum*) came on a Tuesday night and featured exactly one caller—and I'm not sure he even meant to dial the show. It was terrible. I bombed.

My first mistake was writing everything out on paper—the opening to the show, every question I was going to ask our rare guests, what I would say as we went to commercial breaks. I was so organized I wrote out a card that said, "Write out a card."

"This is radio," someone on the station's staff finally told me. "You just talk."

From that night forward, I barely took a breath. I talked early, often and loudly. I had an opinion about everything. I was 100 percent right and everyone else was 100 percent wrong. I thought that's what you were supposed to do on the radio: argue . . . pontificate . . . create controversy. And the louder, the better.

But it doesn't work that way. You can't throw fastballs on every pitch. You can't aim the flamethrower at a microphone and hold the trigger for four hours.

Not long after my first forgettable show, I saw Dick Vitale at a basketball game. I mentioned my radio gig and he made the mistake of not instantly walking away.

So I called him and kept him on the air for an hour. We didn't have any other callers. We didn't have any other guests. And Vitale was too polite to say no. Thirty years later, he's still the kindest guest I've ever had.

Little by little, I developed a voice on radio. I was paid $100 per show for being moderately crummy. Looking back, I was probably overpaid.

Because the seven p.m. slot isn't much of a draw, we would go entire hours without callers. I would give the studio phone number and we'd get nothing. We didn't have a hot line; we had a cold line.

Desperate times required desperate measures.

One night I gave the studio number and, as usual, the switchboard remained unlit. I pleaded again, and again nothing.

"Folks, I want to thank you for your patience," I said. "Our phone lines have been jammed all night and I'm sure you're tired of hearing a busy signal every time you call. But we just opened up another line, so give us a try and we'll see if we can squeeze you in."

And then someone called. And someone after that. By pretending to be popular with callers, we sort of became . . . popular with callers.

Sometimes I would just gig the listeners and see how they'd react. If it was a slow night (which it usually was), I'd invent something like this: "You know, I remember when Bear Bryant was coaching in the Sugar Bowl, and I found it odd that he wore his cap indoors for the game."

The switchboard would light up like it was the Grotto at Notre

Dame. Bama fans would call en masse to tell me I was wrong about the Bear. His momma had taught him proper, they said. The man never wore a hat indoors.

I knew that. But I needed callers. I had to provoke instant reaction. For example, I'd say that Joey Jones had caught a touchdown pass against so-and-so in 19-whatever, even though Joey Jones wasn't even on the team then. A cheap trick? Absolutely.

I respect anyone who does local radio because I know how hard and humbling it can be. It's a cutthroat business. Your existence depends on the station manager, on the ratings and on your willingness to try the unusual.

There were times when we would do the show from a hot dog stand. Think about that for a moment.

I did a show at a car wash. At a tire dealership. At sports bars. At a dog track. At a casino. At a bowling alley. At an optometrist's office. At a disco, which is a lot of fun if you like the Bee Gees, Donna Summer and strobe lights.

In short, if you had an electrical outlet and a folding chair, we could make it work.

The only place I refused to do a show was at a local strip club. Nothing against strippers, but it would have been difficult to conduct a serious interview with, say, the commissioner of the SEC while in the background you heard the Divinyls singing "I Touch Myself," followed by the emcee screaming, "And nowwwwww, let's have a warm Cheetah Lounge welcome for our pole dance queen, Cinnamon!"

My career had taken a bizarre detour. From political science major to dog tracks. From dreams of the *New York Times* to the realities of the *Birmingham Post-Herald* and local radio. I wasn't exactly who I thought I would be.

Writing never came easily for me. As Red Smith, the Pulitzer Prize–winning sports columnist at the *New York Times*, put it: "Writing is easy. You just open a vein and bleed."

I opened an artery. I had a fistfight with every word I typed. I was a perfectionist, but not a perfect writer. I would see other sportswriters crank out lyrical, thoroughly reported and nuanced columns on deadline. Meanwhile, I would obsess over every phrase and comma and lurch toward an uninspired finish. I had my moments—columns I'm incredibly proud of—but it was a battle.

It was the same with radio during those early years. I was learning the job by trial and error, mostly error.

There was a point early in my career when I almost walked away from everything. I was burning out on newspapers and radio seemed better off without me.

I met the dean of Birmingham's Cumberland School of Law at a party. I told him I had always wanted to be a lawyer, and he strongly encouraged me to consider the career switch. And so I decided I would go to law school, take the bar exams and become an accomplished trial attorney.

Linda and I were practically engaged. When I told her about my law school plan she didn't know whether to laugh or leave. She had endured years of undergrad, postgrad and residency and was just beginning her own medical practice. The thought of putting our life on hold as I went through three years of law school didn't appeal to her. She thought I was crazy.

I really did want to do it. Under any other circumstance, I would have done it. I would have walked away from the media right then. I think I would have been a terrific lawyer. But I loved Linda.

Farewell, torts. Goodbye to what might have been.

When you're first trying to build ratings, you tend to invent little skirmishes. I know I did. I was overly critical of coaches, just to stir it up. I would personally attack people. I got a reputation as a hate-monger, a coach killer. To these charges, I wish to plead guilty.

I'd like to think I've come a long way since then.

You have to understand the context to understand why I was so hard on Ray Perkins, Johnny Majors and Pat Dye at the time. I was trying to create a radio persona. I was trying to make the show compelling, relevant and a destination point. And sure, I was trying to get noticed. If that meant I had to hammer a coach or an athletic director, then I'd do it; I wouldn't even think twice about it. And fans—Bama fans, in particular—didn't think twice about throwing beers or batteries at me when I was covering a game at Legion Field.

My strategy worked to some extent. The ratings started to reflect the impact of my columns and my callers. Management noticed too. So did my savings account.

My mom didn't know what to make of it. I called to give her a State of Paul Address in 1990: I had the full-time radio gig. I was writing the lead sports column at the *Post-Herald*. I had reached a career milestone in salary. Life was good.

And then, on December 13, 1994, my mother died. She was a tough, uncompromising woman who had dealt with difficult times. She could find fault with the *Mona Lisa*, but I always knew I could depend on her. And if she were alive today, she'd say something like, "Why can't you wear a nice pocket square like that handsome Herbstreit man?"

And you know what? She would be right. I miss her every day.

On May 13, 2000—the day before Mother's Day—I wrote a column about my mom. Nearly six years had passed since her death, but that didn't make it any easier to put words to paper.

In the column, I told the story of a local magazine writer who had described my upbringing as less than fortunate. In the profile piece he had written: "Paul was abandoned as a child and raised by wolves."

Well, momma wolf demanded I give her the writer's phone number and address. For the writer's sake, I declined.

I wrote about her fondness for Memphis State basketball and especially Memphis State basketball coach Gene Bartow. I wrote about her unauthorized trips into arena media rooms (I would bring her to games), where she would complain about the selection of free fruit. I wrote about some of the first words she ever uttered to my wife-to-be ("I just want you to know right away that I hate women doctors," she announced to Linda, the woman doctor). I wrote about how she would call me in press boxes around the country and complain about the football telecasts.

I recalled the January 26, 1983, day that Bryant died. I was writing the lead story for the *Post-Herald* and was under crushing deadline pressure. Nothing mattered, including the phone that kept ringing on my desk. I ignored it, but a colleague in the newsroom had had enough. He picked up the phone, started to say something and then simply handed me the receiver.

It was my mother calling from Memphis.

"Well, I didn't know if you knew it or not," she said, "but I just saw on Channel 5 that Bear Bryant had died."

Even now, I smile just thinking about that conversation.

I ended the column with this:

" . . . I always remember a picture of *Whistler's Mother* that hung in our kitchen and the saying right below:

IT IS A WONDERFUL THING, A MOTHER;

OTHER FOLKS CAN LOVE YOU,

BUT ONLY YOUR MOTHER UNDERSTANDS,

SHE WORKS FOR YOU,

LOOKS AFTER YOU,

LOVES YOU,

FORGIVES YOU ANYTHING YOU MAY DO,

UNDERSTANDS YOU, AND THEN, THE

ONLY THING BAD SHE EVER DOES TO YOU,

IS TO DIE AND LEAVE YOU.

As the popularity of the radio show grew (we signed a new deal in 2001), the health of the *Post-Herald* declined. The paper was in a free fall. Circulation and advertising were down, and morale was in negative integers.

I was disillusioned by the decline, mostly because nobody was reading the paper. In other words, nobody was reading me, or anyone else in our sports department. The *Post-Herald* was a shadow of its shadow.

So I resigned. It wasn't a decision made easily. After all, I had spent more than twenty years in the newspaper business. I was a newspaperman—and proud of it. The *Post-Herald*, for all of its flaws, had helped me establish a presence in Birmingham.

My retirement from newspapers lasted exactly two days. I quit on a Wednesday. Regretted it on a Thursday. On Friday the editor of the *Mobile Register* called and said, "Would you like to write columns for us?"

"Sure," I said.

And that was that. For the next ten years I wrote two columns a week for the *Register*. The column found its way online onto AL.com, which exposed me to a new audience.

In keeping with my history of dying newspapers (remember the *Philly Journal* and the *Nashville Banner?*), the *Post-Herald* quit publishing in September 2005. By then, the daily circulation had fallen below 10,000.

As the radio show got bigger, so did the number of listeners in other parts of the state. We started getting calls not just from the Birmingham area, but from Huntsville, Mobile, Montgomery and points in between.

Then, in 2002, came a huge break for us. The *Tennessean*, in Nashville, published a poll ranking the Most Influential People in the SEC. I came in fourth.

I had no idea how they did the polling and I didn't care. We came in fourth! For a mom-and-pop show stuck in faraway Birmingham, it was like finishing first. I don't know if No. 4 in a *Tennessean* poll is a big deal, but we made it into a big deal.

C'mon? Me?

I wasn't going to argue with the results. We started promoting it: *Paul Finebaum—Mr. SEC.*

Then, in 2004, *Sports Illustrated* listed its top twelve sports talk shows in America. We were on the list. I think even my mom would have been impressed by that one. Anyway, we'll promote that on the show until the end of time.

Everything really began to change in 2007. I moved to WJOX and we never looked back. We never had to worry about anything other than making the show better.

I'd like to take all the credit for the show's success, but I can't. That's because the person who made the biggest impact on our show wasn't employed by WJOX, but by the University of Alabama. His name: Nicholas Lou "Nick" Saban.

About two weeks before I joined the station, Bama hired Saban away from the Miami Dolphins. The first year was difficult for Saban. Bama lost to Louisiana-Monroe, which seems almost incomprehensible today, but nothing spurs discussion quite like a loss.

As Saban turned around the program, we started to attract a larger audience. The more Bama won, the more callers and listeners came to the show. We were like the local pizza joint that Zagat makes into a tourist attraction. It was exciting—not just for me, but for our callers. *My* show wasn't going national—*OUR* show was going national.

You now could hear us from coast to coast. A show about the SEC had become a hit from L.A. to Boston. Take a bow, SEC.

Truth is, I was in the right place at the right time. I was in the right conference, the right city, covering the right university, the right coach and the right rivalry. I rode the coattails of Saban's success, but I'll give myself some credit for predicting that success. I thought he would win national championships—and I said so early on.

It helped that Saban was willing to give me the time of day. That wasn't always the case with Alabama coaches. Ray Perkins once got me fired at a Birmingham radio station.

It also helped that Herbstreit, CBS's Gary Danielson and other national figures were regulars on the show. They gave the show some gravitas and credibility. Our callers (we probably take a hundred-plus calls per day) gave it its soul. I gave it some teeth.

I picked my spots, of course. I never got behind the microphone and thought, "OK, what coach can I get fired today?"

That was never the purpose of the show. Certainly I've written stories and columns that might have influenced a decision. But as far as the radio show, no, I don't think the show has ever wielded that kind of power.

For example, Mike Price got fired from Alabama because he was an idiot and indiscreet.

Mike Shula got fired from Alabama because he lost to Mississippi State.

Gene Chizik got fired from Auburn because he lost to everyone.

Did the show sometimes mirror the prevailing attitude of the fans? Absolutely. Did those views help nudge an athletic director, school president or board of trustees toward making a decision? Probably.

Why isn't there a Paul Finebaum of the Big Ten, ACC, etc.? That's easy—because in the SEC we talk about only one sport all year round. We'll dip into other topics, but college football is what we do best.

I remember when we did our first show on SiriusXM. The first caller wanted to know if I thought the NCAA Selection Committee should make Temple a No. 4 or 5 seed for the hoops tournament.

I didn't know if Temple should have been a No. 4 or 5 seed because I didn't care. It wasn't interesting radio. I'm not sure it would have been interesting even to the Temple basketball team. So we moved on to the next caller, preferably one who wanted to talk about football.

When Oregon played Auburn for the BCS Championship in early January of 2011, I found myself talking to Bill Hancock in the University of Phoenix Stadium press box shortly before kickoff. Hancock is the spokesperson and executive director of the BCS and the new playoff system. You've seen him in the past—he hands the crystal trophy to the national championship coach. In other words, you've seen him in a lot of photos with Saban.

The guy has run fifteen marathons. He has ridden his bicycle across the USA twice. He helped run the Final Four.

He's done stuff. And he's also endured stuff, such as the death of his thirty-one-year-old son Will, an Oklahoma State media relations official who died in a January 27, 2001, plane crash that also claimed the lives of OSU players, staffers and the flight crew of the charter plane.

Bill and I chatted that night. He said, "Tell me about your career."

So I gave him the cheat sheet version. I told him that my career had plateaued. I had done fine—maybe better than fine—but that my best days were probably behind me. I was successful, but not in the way I had envisioned.

Bill looked at me with sort of a wry smile and a semi-incredulous look on his face.

"Paul, what are you talking about?" he said. "Don't you realize where you are right now?"

And I guess I didn't.

I have been told numerous times throughout my career that I would never make it in radio. I was told enough times that I began to believe it. I don't hold a grudge, but I do remember those who believed in me. And Birmingham believed in me. The South believed in me.

So here I am, a New Yorker by DNA, but a Southerner by birth certificate, driver's license and home address. Or as one of my callers puts it, I'm "a carpetbagging son of a pissant."

I'm not exactly sure how or why I got here—here being the South and on radio and TV—but I've never left. I've had my chances, but there's a certain gravitational pull that keeps me where I am. One of these days, I'll even use the word "Y'all."

I've always known the SEC is the best. The Big Ten people have finally come to admit that. And I know I sound like one of those crazed talk show callers, but I honestly feel like I could step in and be Paul's sidekick on the radio and make the show better.

—JEFF FROM CHICAGO

CHAPTER 9

Urban and Paul = BFFs

Saturday, October 5, 2013
Evanston, Illinois

THE SEASON SKINNY: Georgia rallies to beat Tennessee in overtime, but loses a running back, two wide receivers and a punter during the win. . . . Unranked Auburn defeats Ole Miss, the Tigers' first win against a Top 25 team in two years. . . . Bama safety Ha Ha Clinton-Dix misses the win against Georgia State after being suspended indefinitely for accepting a short-term loan from a Tide assistant strength and conditioning coach. . . . After beating Northwestern tonight, Ohio State has only one game remaining against a team currently ranked in the AP poll (Michigan).

You know whom I really miss in the SEC?

Urban Meyer.

I miss how he grated on other SEC coaches' nerves. I miss the drama he created. I miss his paranoia. His passion. His intensity.

I don't miss his parsing of words. His cryptic responses to simple, direct questions. His Urban vs. The World mentality.

I guarantee you that the other SEC coaches are glad he left Florida after the 2010 season. That's because he outworked, outcoached and outrecruited most of them. He also annoyed them. According to those who were in the room during the annual spring SEC coaches' meetings, Meyer could be combative, abrasive and unendurable at times.

Meyer wasn't there to make friends. He certainly wasn't buddies with Lane Kiffin, who once wrongly accused Meyer of cheating. His relationship with most of the other coaches in the SEC, such as South Carolina's Spurrier, was, at best, cordial, professional and a little on the icy side.

GameDay is at Northwestern today. So is Meyer and his undefeated Buckeyes.

Big Ten coaches have quickly learned that Meyer is relentless in his pursuit of winning championships. Ohio State's hiring him was just as important to the future of Buckeyes football as the hiring of Saban was at Alabama. You'll see.

I love when his former SEC peers say things like, "Well, anybody could have won with Tim Tebow at quarterback." Or, "It's Florida— you're supposed to win national championships there." Or, "He left Florida when the going got tough."

Sure, from a pure leadership standpoint, Tebow might have been the greatest college quarterback in the history of the game. We can agree on that, can't we? He willed teams to victory. He was an inside-the-tackles rushing nightmare, a red zone mismatch, and even with his funky, mechanically flawed throwing motion, he kept defenses honest with his passing game.

He also had the perfect coach in Meyer, whose first national championship at Florida came in 2006 with Chris Leak, not Tebow, at quarterback. Leak went undrafted in 2007 and never played a down in the NFL. He was a talented college quarterback, but Meyer squeezed the best out of him.

Tebow led the Gators to the national title in 2008 after winning a Heisman in 2007. He got drafted in the first round by the Denver Broncos in 2010. I'm sure you've followed the ups and downs of his pro career since then.

The point is, he did his best work under Meyer. Leak did his best work under Meyer. Ohio State quarterback Braxton Miller has done his best work under Meyer. Those aren't coincidences.

Meyer quit Florida because of stress-related problems, sat out a year and then magically recovered (so say UF fans) in time to take the Ohio State job. Or maybe Gator fans are mad that he led an NCAA-sanctioned Buckeyes team to an undefeated season in 2012, and left Evanston tonight with the win against the Wildcats to remain unbeaten.

Meyer was named after a pope, but he's no saint. Despite his flaws—and he'll be the first to tell you about them—I found it utterly ridiculous when Meyer-bashers tried to connect the dots between his tenure at Florida and the alleged criminal actions of former Gators/New England Patriots tight end Aaron Hernandez.

As tempting as it is to blame Meyer for everything that's gone wrong with mankind, you can't blame him for Hernandez's being charged with murder in June 2013. If you do, then when do you start pointing the finger at Patriots head coach Bill Belichick? Or Hernandez's high school coach? You don't.

Did Meyer run a loose ship at times at Florida? Yes. Did he let things get a bit out of control? Yes. But it's just insane to say Meyer could have prevented Hernandez from following the path he allegedly followed later in life. To think so is to give football coaches too much credit.

If you talk with those who know Meyer best, they'll tell you the same thing: that Meyer might have cared *too* much. When a player made an off-field mistake, Meyer took it hard. The player's failure was Meyer's failure.

I spent time with Meyer several years ago at a party in Scottsdale, Arizona, when Auburn was playing for the BCS Championship against Oregon. I didn't want to like him, but I walked away thinking that there was a good and decent person underneath the steely demeanor.

Don't misunderstand me: I wouldn't want to go on an Alaskan cruise with him. He'd be the kind of guy who would turn the nightly ballroom dancing into a competition. He'd insist on two-a-day practices for shuffleboard.

In 2011, the year he sat out of coaching and worked for ESPN as an analyst, I stood next to him during parts of the Alabama-LSU game in Tuscaloosa. No. 1 LSU vs. No. 2 Bama. It was that year's Game of the Century.

In my years around football coaches, I've never seen a more tortured guy than Meyer as he watched the Tide and the Tigers play that night. He was a mere spectator to a huge game and you could tell it was driving him nuts. He needed to be in the middle of it. He needed to be on the sidelines, with a headset, with a result in the balance.

It didn't surprise me that he sat out only one year. Had Ohio State not been available, I think he would have taken another job. There's no way he would have survived a second consecutive season without coaching football. He's a coach and always will be a coach. That's what he was born to do.

It also doesn't surprise me that he has rebuilt the Ohio State program in such a short time. The NCAA sanctions (scholarship reductions, as well as a 2012 postseason ban) left a deep bruise, but they weren't fatal.

I used to think the Big 12 would be the conference with the best chance of unseating the SEC and becoming master of the college football domain. I bought into the theory that Texas and Oklahoma were the Alabama and LSU of their league, that Baylor was Georgia, Oklahoma State was Florida, Kansas State was Auburn, etc. I thought Bob Stoops and Mack Brown could go on a run and take turns winning national championships.

But who was I kidding? Stoops hasn't won a national title since 2000, Brown since 2005. The two conferences don't compare.

The one conference that could eventually challenge the SEC is the Big Ten. The league has mostly been a nonfactor in the BCS Era, but it has the infrastructure to be competitive in the future. It has a strong commissioner in Delany and a very valuable property in the Big Ten Network. The conference has a wide recruiting base, stretching from the Midwest to the Mid-Atlantic to the Northeast. And it can cherry-pick in Florida too.

Most of all, it has Ohio State and Michigan, as well as a solid supporting cast in Michigan State, Nebraska, Wisconsin, Iowa and, when the NCAA sanctions finally end, Penn State.

It has good coaches and one great one: Meyer. He's won national championships in the toughest college conference on the planet. He knows what it takes to succeed. His attention to detail is Sabanesque, or maybe it's the other way around.

Now he's at a program, much like when he was at Florida, where everything is designed for success. You have every advantage, every facility, every recruiting base, every resource to win. And Urban Meyer is not going to be intimidated by any other program or any other coach.

Think back to the SEC in 2008, when Meyer's Gators won their second national championship in three years. Four of the SEC teams he beat that season were coached by men with national title rings: Tennessee's Phillip Fulmer, LSU's Miles, South Carolina's Spurrier and Bama's Saban. Add the late-season victory against Florida State's Bobby Bowden, and the BCS Championship win against Oklahoma's Stoops, and Meyer defeated six guys who had won national titles.

Plus, think about the second tier of coaches in the SEC that year: Arkansas's Petrino, Georgia's Richt, Auburn's Tuberville, Kentucky's Rich Brooks and 2007 SEC Coach of the Year Sylvester Croom of Mississippi State.

I've always been intrigued by the personalities of the ultrasuccessful coaches. Meyer is hyperintense, to the point that the pressures of the job overwhelmed him and he had to walk away from the game. His family wouldn't let him return to coaching unless he agreed to a ten-point contract (written by one of his daughters) promising to restructure his approach to the day-to-day demands of the job. He signed it, and a framed copy hangs on a wall behind his desk at Ohio State.

Now compare him with Spurrier, who is hypercompetitive, but not self-destructive in the way Meyer was before he quit at Florida. Spurrier wants to win, but he doesn't *need* to win. His programs, from Duke to Florida to South Carolina, have always had a more relaxed feel to them. The children of his assistant coaches roam the office hallways. Nobody is expected to pull all-nighters and sleep on couches. You get your work done and then you go home to see your family at a decent hour. It isn't a gulag.

When Spurrier speaks with the media, anything is possible. He can be glib, biting, sarcastic, opinionated—sometimes all in the same interview—but is rarely dull.

Meyer isn't glib. He doesn't yuk it up. He doesn't pose for impromptu photos in front of the condiment counter at Arby's, as Spurrier did after appearing at this year's SEC Media Days. He doesn't go shirtless like Spurrier. Meyer coaches intense and talks intense. He chooses his words as carefully as he chooses a third-down play.

After tonight's entertaining 40–30 Ohio State victory against Northwestern, Meyer provides the typical boilerplate postgame comments. He compliments the Wildcats' effort (Northwestern was in the game until the final minutes) and their offensive scheme. He is gracious and calculated. He can afford to be—the Buckeyes have only one game remaining on their regular-season schedule against a team presently ranked in the top 25 (Michigan).

Meanwhile, his old SEC foe Spurrier has had a more eventful day. In fact, what is unfolding in Columbia, South Carolina, after today's victory against Kentucky is much more interesting than what happened here in Evanston.

The real news of the day has nothing to do with Spurrier's twentieth career win against UK's Wildcats, or with the Gamecocks' fourteen-game home winning streak.

Instead, it has everything to do with defensive end Jadeveon Clowney, only the second-most hyped college football player in the country. Clowney entered YouTube lore with his tackle/near-decapitation of a Michigan running back in the Gamecocks' bowl game in January. I remember watching the play in the Outback Bowl and wondering if the head of Vincent Smith was still in the helmet that had flown six yards backwards after the hit.

Clowney was the SEC Freshman of the Year in 2011. He finished sixth in the 2012 Heisman Trophy balloting, a season in which he set school records in sacks and tackles for losses. If he declares for the NFL Draft after this season (a foregone conclusion), he is considered the likely choice for the No. 1 overall pick.

But for all of Clowney's well-documented physical skills, there are rumblings about his work ethic and motivation. Those rumblings were given credence in South Carolina's season-opening win against North Carolina.

Clowney played as if he were dragging a ninety-pound barbell. He took plays off. He jogged. He looked like he needed an oxygen machine.

The official explanation was that Clowney had battled a stomach virus earlier that week. I don't think the Head Ball Coach bought into it.

"Did you watch what I was watching?" said Spurrier when asked about Clowney's performance that day.

Spurrier's message was clear: Clowney's conditioning was subpar.

There were even more questions about Clowney after today's blowout victory against Kentucky. Shortly before kickoff, Clowney had stunned Spurrier and the team by announcing he wasn't going to play because of bruised ribs. As soon as I heard the news, I knew this had the makings of a huge story. Clowney had been nursing the injury, but nobody, including Spurrier, thought he would call in sick for the UK game.

Spurrier isn't good at hiding his emotions. I can see that tonight while watching the highlights of his postgame press conference on ESPN. It is obvious that Spurrier is annoyed and maybe feeling a little betrayed by Clowney's surprise decision, and that the Gamecocks will move on with or without their star defensive end.

Once again, Clowney's work ethic is an issue. Is Clowney jaking it? Is Clowney protecting himself for the NFL Draft? Is Spurrier enabling him? Has there been some colossal miscommunication between Clowney, the South Carolina athletic training staff and Spurrier?

Whatever it is, it threatens to unhinge South Carolina's season if it isn't corrected, and corrected fast.

Of course, I can't wait to talk about this on Monday's show. I've also been invited to appear on an ESPNU roundtable to discuss Clowney's latest actions. He isn't going to like what I have to say.

Paul Finebaum has been the epitome of
insignificance for many decades.

—SOUTH CAROLINA FOOTBALL MESSAGE BOARD

CHAPTER 10

On Second Thought . . .

Saturday, October 12, 2013
Seattle, Washington

THE SEASON SKINNY: Utah upsets Stanford on Thursday night. . . . South Carolina destroys Arkansas, 52–7, prompting Spurrier to tell reporters, "That's no fun getting your butt beat at home–homecoming and all that." . . . Missouri upsets Georgia. . . . Texas crushes Oklahoma, providing Mack Brown a reprieve from his many Longhorn critics. . . . Former U.S. secretary of state Condoleezza Rice is expected to be named to the College Football Playoff's selection committee, an announcement that causes former Auburn head coach Pat Dye to helpfully point out, "To understand football, you've got to play with your hand in the dirt."

I t isn't often that you come face-to-face with the coach you once compared on national television to Miley Cyrus. Even rarer is to endure that indignity on the same day an athletic director on the other side of the country piles on and suggests that you're a fraud.

But here I am, Paul Finebaum, holding the exacta ticket from hell.

I've made the cross-country trip to Seattle for *GameDay*'s visit to Washington, where No. 16 U-Dub is playing second-ranked Oregon. I'm jet-lagged and stressed. A middle seat, in the last row of the plane, bracketed by three crying babies during the five-and-a-half-hour Friday flight didn't help.

And then I find out Lane Kiffin is going to be on the show. It is going to be his first public interview since his firing. It will also be our first in-person encounter since the infamous Cyrus comparison.

The *GameDay* production office is housed in an administrative building just off Washington's Red Square. It is in Red Square, with the school's gorgeous Suzzallo Library in the background, where we will do the show.

When Kiffin walks into our *GameDay* meeting room, there is only one thing for me to do: shake hands and introduce myself. I don't know what to expect in return. But Kiffin is gracious, disarming and even friendly. If he harbors any anger over my Cyrus comments, he doesn't show it. What I thought might be an awkward moment isn't awkward at all. In fact, it's actually pleasant.

Kiffin and I spend time after our TV hits and chat about his future. I walk away from our encounter wondering if getting fired by USC has somehow changed him for the better. Because this isn't the same tone-deaf Kiffin who had casually jilted Tennessee, or alienated the USC decision makers and key members of the Los Angeles media. This Kiffin has personality, a sense of humor and a sense of humility.

In its own way, being on *GameDay* is teaching me lessons, too. On radio, you sometimes criticize in the vacuum of an isolated studio. But because of the reach and seeming monopoly of *GameDay*, some of the people I have criticized—Manziel . . . Kiffin—become three-dimensional. How did someone put it? *The power of proximity.*

What I had said about Manziel and Kiffin wasn't personal. In fact, that's exactly what I tell Kiffin—that it wasn't personal. I'm paid to offer an educated opinion. I take that responsibility seriously.

But sometimes my opinion can be better phrased and better framed. That doesn't mean I'm going to retreat from a controversial topic. And if I think someone has done wrong, I'm going to say so. But no college coach deserves to be compared to the Queen of Twerk. I made a mistake, and tried to convey that to Kiffin.

I exchange cell numbers with Kiffin and we promise to keep in touch. (He later texts me to say he enjoyed our conversation and had just listened to "Wrecking Ball" by Cyrus. He said he laughed when he heard it.) I didn't know what his future held. No major or even mid-major college program was going to hand him another head coaching job, so he was going to have to become an offensive coordinator or position coach again. Maybe he could return to the NFL as an assistant.

For a variety of reasons—some due to the cumulative effect of NCAA sanctions levied against USC when Pete Carroll led the Trojans—Kiffin had failed at his dream job. He had lost the confidence of his athletic director and didn't have enough equity with the movers and shakers of the program to survive the tough times. I wish him the best—and I mean it.

Kiffin and I are cool with each other. But I have apparently made more enemies than I realize.

Earlier in the week, I had been part of an ESPNU roundtable discussion about Jadeveon Clowney. I hit Clowney the same way Clowney had hit the Michigan running back in the Outback Bowl.

"I think his demeanor this year, starting at North Carolina, has been disgraceful," I said on the program. "And I think he is clearly the biggest joke in college football right now. The biggest joke in college football from the opening game until now. People are laughing at this guy."

I added that Spurrier had helped create the situation.

The bite was replayed on *SportsCenter*, and the quotes were tweeted out by ESPNU.

The facts are that Clowney has massively underachieved in 2013, and that he and Spurrier appear to have serious communication issues. Questioning a player's health is dicey business—if he's truly hurt, he's hurt. But I'm questioning Clowney's desire to play college football. He is acting like a guy who is counting the minutes until the NFL Draft, a guy trying to decide what to do when he meets NFL commissioner Roger Goodell on the Radio City Music Hall stage: handshake or man-hug?

Not long after my appearance on ESPNU, I got a call from Spurrier. He wasn't pleased.

"You guys are the ones who said Clowney was the best," said Spurrier, referring to the media's image-making capabilities.

True. We have helped create the myth that is Clowney. And South Carolina has been a willing partner. But I also can read a stat sheet, and it is impossible to ignore the drop-off in Clowney's on-field production. By any reasonable measurement, he is having an un-Clowney-like season. At the pace he is on, Clowney is going to be lucky to finish the regular season with a half dozen sacks and double-digit tackles for losses.

Spurrier is doing his best to spackle over the controversy. He said earlier in the week that every Gamecock, "including me . . . we need to be appreciative that [Clowney] chose South Carolina." He added, "He is hurt. If he doesn't play another down, every Gamecock should be thankful he is here."

Thankful? I think that's a bit too much. Clowney is a gifted player, but he hasn't transformed the South Carolina program. He has strengthened it. Increased the national awareness of it. Helped the team win a few more games. But they aren't going to build a statue of him outside Williams-Brice Stadium.

I understand why Spurrier is doing damage control. By publicly supporting Clowney, he diffuses the situation and keeps his best player from completely disengaging from the team. It is a pragmatic move made in the best interests of Clowney (Spurrier could have gone negative and jeopardized the defensive end's draft standing), and in the best interests of the Gamecocks (a semimotivated and interested Clowney is better than no Clowney at all).

But I'm not completely buying Spurrier's conciliatory tone. He was upset in the aftermath of Clowney's last-second decision not to play against Kentucky. He's still upset (and had a discussion with Clowney in a private meeting); he's just hiding it better.

South Carolina athletic director Ray Tanner isn't hiding *his* feelings today. Someone just sent me a link to a tweet that quotes Tanner ripping me for my recent criticism of Clowney. Several other members of the *GameDay* crew have it seen it too.

Here's the quote from Tanner's pregame appearance on the Gamecock IMG Sports Network: "I'm OK with scrutiny, I'm OK with calling it like you see it, whether it's the offense, the defense or whatever the case may be," said Tanner on the pregame show. "But this week when Paul Finebaum . . . . I think he was quoted as saying Jadeveon Clowney's the biggest joke in college football—that was too much for me. That was unprofessional, that was unnecessary, it was inappropriate."

In short, I think Mr. Tanner hopes I remain permanently in Seattle and pursue a career as a Starbucks barista or, better yet, work on a fishing trawler and, in a perfect world, be lost at sea.

As a parting shot, Tanner says he has concerns about my upcoming role on the soon-to-be-launched SEC Network.

I'm used to people firing back at me; it comes with the territory. But Tanner's response hurts, not because I think I'm entirely wrong about Clowney, but because I'm beginning to wonder if my brand of acerbic opinion translates to TV.

I don't criticize college players on a regular basis. I think there's a certain truth to the idea that they're not professional players so you give them the benefit of the doubt. But there are exceptions, and in Clowney we're talking about the early-consensus choice for the No. 1 pick in the NFL. He is a professional-in-waiting. He is being scrutinized by coaches, pro scouts, opponents, the media and fans. To pretend he is your ordinary college player would be ridiculous. When he had chosen South Carolina out of high school, there was nearly a flash party in Columbia. He wasn't ordinary then; he isn't ordinary in 2013.

Tanner is defending one of his own. No problem. But if you're going to call me unprofessional and call my comments inappropriate, then it has to be for better reasons than hurt feelings.

In the context of the 2013 season and in the context of the expectations South Carolina's own coaching staff had for Clowney, his level of play *is* a major disappointment. His conditioning and effort against North Carolina in the opener had been a joke. The would-be Heisman candidate/best college defensive player in the country/consensus No. 1 NFL Draft pick shouldn't shrug off entire parts of a game. Even his own head coach was clearly unimpressed by the performance—and said so. Was Tanner offended by that?

And how could you not shake your head in amazement at the way Clowney handled his decision to sit against Kentucky? He had bruised ribs and didn't feel comfortable playing in a game—fine, no problem. But to wait until the last minute and then essentially say, "Surprise! I'm not playing!" was an insult to his teammates, coaches and fans.

Of course, South Carolina should have been happy someone was even talking about its football program. Spurrier has done an impressive job rebuilding it since his arrival in 2005, but there was a time during his tenure that people—including perhaps the Head Ball Coach himself—wondered if he could undo the inertia of the place.

South Carolina is the most misunderstood program in the SEC. Even with its recent success, Gamecocks football doesn't stop traffic. Spurrier won eleven games in 2011, eleven games in 2012 and could be on his way to double-digit victories in 2013, too. But you never hear the Gamecocks mentioned in the same breath as Bama. It is an under-the-radar program that wins games, wins big recruiting battles, but has yet to break through and win the games that matter most.

Since joining the league, South Carolina has never won an SEC Championship Game (the only one in which they played saw the 'Cocks outscored by 39 points) and has never appeared in a BCS bowl. Until it does, you can't call the Gamecocks an elite SEC program.

In the past, the school was satisfied with being average. Its football goals weren't ambitious enough. If you know one thing about Spurrier, know this: he doesn't do average. He is one of the most competitive people you'll ever meet. I know people say that all the time: *He doesn't want to lose a game of checkers.* Blah, blah, blah.

But Spurrier truly despises losing. He makes millions a year, but he'll fight to the death over a $10 golf bet. He doesn't give gimme putts. He says that if Tiger Woods has to putt them, then so should you. And him.

Spurrier isn't in it for moral victories. There are Wins, Losses and Ties. There isn't a category for Almost Wins, or Losses Where We Should Feel Good About Ourselves. He is a zero-sum type of coach.

Spurrier has won games at South Carolina, but the hardest job has been changing the culture of the place. He has had to condition South Carolina fans, alums, donors and administrators to embrace success and not accept anything less. No cheering after losses, for one thing.

In many ways, I think he has done a better job at South Carolina than he did at Florida. He has made the program relevant. During South Carolina's early SEC years, you barely knew it was in the league.

When the SEC expanded to twelve teams in 1990, I thought it should have invited Florida State and Miami. And when it went to fourteen teams, the next two invitees should have been Texas and Oklahoma. And if you wanted the perfect sixteen-team superconference, then you would have added Clemson and Texas A&M.

But it didn't work out that way. The SEC thought it had a deal with FSU, but I think Bobby Bowden had some misgivings about joining the league. Perhaps he felt that FSU, a longtime independent, had been disrespected in the past by the SEC, and would be disrespected in the future. And from a practical football standpoint, I think he knew it would be much easier to navigate the ACC than the SEC. I can see him saying to himself, "I already play Florida every year, why do I want to add Georgia, Tennessee and the rest of them? I can go to the ACC and beat up on them little fellers." So he took his program to the ACC, and he proved to be correct.

With FSU off the table, SEC commissioner Roy Kramer had to scramble. It had invited Arkansas as the eleventh member and ulti-mately decided on South Carolina as the twelfth.

At the time, I was underwhelmed. I didn't see how South Carolina fit into the SEC footprint. And Arkansas had almost as many head coaches in its inaugural season (two) as it did wins (three). The Gamecocks weren't much better. They finished 5-6.

During that 1992 season, I saw Bama beat Arkansas by 27 on the road and beat South Carolina by 41 at home. These were the two new proud members of the SEC?

Roy Kramer knew he had gotten the runts of the litter, but he was committed to Arkansas and South Carolina for better or worse. And what, he was going to kick the two teams out of the SEC because Finebaum said so? Maybe. I wrote a column comparing the loss of FSU and the acquisition of South Carolina to getting dumped by Julia Roberts— and marrying Roseanne Barr.

South Carolina fans didn't smile. The following year, when Bama traveled to Columbia for an early October game, I could see "Kill Finebaum" signs at the stadium.

Spurrier's hiring in 2005 was a godsend for the program, made possible by Daniel Snyder, the impatient Washington Redskins owner who had fired the Head Ball Coach after just two seasons (12-20) in D.C. An unemployed Spurrier cashed Snyder's buyout money in 2004 and then returned to the SEC after Lou Holtz departed from Columbia.

Only a few months after his hiring, more than $3 million worth of donations flooded in to the athletic department. The newspaper of record in South Carolina, the *State*, began to run a daily update called, "Countdown to the Spurrier Era."

Or as some reporters were calling it: "Return of the Visor."

There were more credentials issued for the 2005 SEC Media Days (nearly 700) than had been issued for the 2004 SEC Championship Game. There were only about 100 fewer media members there to listen to Spurrier and Co. than there had been at the actual national championship game seven months earlier.

Spurrier's return had energized South Carolina football and given the SEC a nice little jolt. It didn't hurt that Urban Meyer was also making his SEC debut as Florida's new coach, after a successful stint at Utah, or that super-recruiter Ed Orgeron had arrived at Ole Miss, or that a strange, powerful force called Les Miles had replaced Saban at LSU.

Spurrier won a national title, six official SEC Championships (seven, if you count 1990, when the Gators finished first but were ineligible because of NCAA sanctions) and 122 games during his reign at Florida. But he had some heavy lifting to do at South Carolina. On his first tour of the facilities, I hear, he paused in front of the team's meager trophy case and offered a short summation of Gamecock football before he'd even arrived.

"Outback Bowl," said Spurrier flatly. "That's about it."

Spurrier had been at South Carolina for two seasons when Alabama athletic director Mal Moore decided to fire Mike Shula in late 2006. The speculation immediately centered on Saban—who was coaching the NFL's Miami Dolphins and had quickly issued a statement saying he wasn't interested—and Spurrier.

I had a friend whose father had played for the Tide and who was himself a bigwig at the university. He called me shortly after Shula's dismissal.

"Do you think Spurrier would be interested in the job?" asked my friend.

"I really don't know," I said.

"Would you call him for me? Would you call Spurrier?"

Spurrier and I had played golf together a couple times, had broken bread, and talked on a regular basis. But Steve is smart enough to leave some distance between himself and the media.

Meanwhile, I was in an uncomfortable place journalistically—in the middle of an evolving story that I was duty-bound to cover. I now knew that prominent and very influential Alabama people were interested in a back-channel conversation with Spurrier. But the only way I had known that—and the only way I would learn anything else moving forward—was to make the call to Spurrier.

So I decided to contact him. I called and left Spurrier a message: "There's something interesting going on here. I don't know if you're out recruiting, but if you get a minute, call me back."

Spurrier soon returned the call.

I said, "I don't know if you're interested in this or not—and obviously you don't want me as a go-between—but I'm just telling you that Alabama has a lot of interest in you."

Later, my Alabama contact called me and said the school was serious about wanting to hire Spurrier. If Spurrier would take the call, Moore would contact him that night.

So I called Spurrier back and relayed the information.

The next day Spurrier called and said he had decided to remain at South Carolina. He liked Columbia. His family had just moved there. He thought he was on the verge of making over the program.

I didn't try to persuade him, but I did make the point that Alabama, even with its problems at the time, was still one of THE destination spots for a coach who loved winning as much as he did. A Bama at 80 percent was better than a South Carolina at 100 percent.

"Steve, I think Alabama could be a really good job," I said.

"Nah," said Spurrier.

A few days later, Spurrier signed a contract extension at South Carolina. (As a footnote, though, the Gamecocks didn't turn the corner after that 2006 season. Instead, they went from 8-5 to 6-6, the beginning of a three-year stretch in which Spurrier lost six games in each of those seasons. During that same time, Alabama played in two SEC Championships and won a BCS Championship.)

Spurrier has it going now at South Carolina. His recruiting classes are strong. He beats in-state rival Clemson on a regular basis (and gigs Swinney like he used to gig Tennessee's Fulmer). Now he needs to figure out a way to reach another SEC Championship Game (the Gamecocks were last there in 2010).

The most terrifying thought if you're a South Carolina fan: What happens when Spurrier calls it quits? He'll be sixty-nine when the 2014 season begins. He looks and acts twenty years younger, but the simple truth is that he can't go on forever. In fact, he's coached longer than I thought he would.

The minute he retires is the minute South Carolina faces a program-defining decision. And when it happens, Tanner will have more important things to worry about than me and Clowney.

Tito Puente is gonna be dead and you're going to say,
"Oh, I've been listening to him for years and I think he's
fantastic."

—BILL MURRAY IN *STRIPES*

CHAPTER 11

The Little Acorn That Becomes the Oak

Saturday, October 19, 2013
Clemson, South Carolina

THE SEASON SKINNY: Two weeks until LSU-BAMA . . . the No. 11 Game-cocks lose to Tennessee; Georgia loses to Vandy. . . . UCF upsets Louisville as the Teddy Bridgewater Heisman Trophy campaign takes a hit. . . . Florida State redshirt freshman quarterback Jameis Winston, a no-show on the preseason Heisman list, zooms into contention as the Seminoles face off with Clem-son. . . . The College Football Playoff's selection committee is officially intro-duced (aside from Condi, it includes Andrew Luck's dad). . . . Bama's Clinton-Dix is reinstated by the NCAA in time for tonight's game against Arkansas.

Florida State exposes the Tigers for what they are—national cham-pionship pretenders—and does so in a big way. The more I watch FSU, the more I'm impressed. I'm so impressed I've decided it wouldn't lose more than two or three games if it played in the SEC.

In the first AP top-five matchup of the season, the Seminoles win, 51–14, and I'm not sure it was that close. FSU actually did Clemson a favor. Might as well lose now and get it over with rather than wait until November 30, when South Carolina will probably do to Clemson what Charles from Reeltown always threatens to do to me: that is, administer a country-boy ass whuppin'.

Speaking of whuppin', Bill Murray made *GameDay* history today when he became the first guest picker to register a takedown of Coach Corso on live television. You knew Murray would do something out of the ordinary (while playing in the AT&T Pebble Beach National Pro-Am,

Murray has been known to make sand angels in the bunkers . . . and to win the Pro-Am championship), but nobody expected him to gently wrestle Coach to the ground. You'll have to YouTube it, because I can't describe it.

I also can't describe what it was like to finish my last hit, dash to the *GameDay* bus to get out of the morning drizzle, and find one of the biggest stars of my generation watching the show with his son. It was one of those moments when you say to yourself, "I'm on a bus with Bill Murray. How is this possible?"

I've met famous people. I don't usually fall to pieces. Usually.

But Murray is one of my all-time favorites. I couldn't help it—I became the archetypical fan

Before I could say anything, he stood up, extended his hand and said, "Paul, Bill Murray."

As he said my name, I was thinking, "How would he know me?"

Duh—he had just seen my *GameDay* hit on one of the monitors on the bus.

I said all the predictable things: I was a huge fan . . . I loved his work. And the whole time I could see him giving me the once-over, trying to size me up. He knew why Desmond, Chris, David, Coach and Kirk were on *GameDay*. Me, he wasn't sure about.

"How'd you get on the show?" he said, not unkindly.

"I was a writer," I said. "Now I have a radio show. For some reason they were looking for a balding, nerdy-looking, middle-aged guy."

He kind of laughed.

I had recently been to New York, so I mentioned something about *Ghostbusters*, which was filmed there thirty years earlier. We talked about golf, so I felt compelled to say something about *Caddyshack*. Thank goodness I hadn't been to Japan, or I would have said something about his golf swing (sweet) in *Lost in Translation*.

As soon as the show was done, I texted two of my friends and said, "You'll never believe who I just met," which was stupid, since the show was on, you know, national television. So they had a pretty good idea who I had just met.

Whatever. It was a stop-and-smell-the-roses moment for me. It has also been a long week for me. The fallout over my Clowney comments has taken a toll. But as silly as it sounds, meeting Murray and watching him wrestle a seventy-eight-year-old man to the floor of the *GameDay* set makes it all better.

Maybe Murray can help Dabo Swinney. He looks like he could use a pick-me-upper, too, after the loss to FSU.

I like Swinney. I like his energy. I like his passion for his program. I like what he's done at Clemson. But Clemson is always good for at least one inexplicable letdown per season. Florida State is a talented team, but to lose by 37 . . . at home . . . on national television . . . with *GameDay* here . . . with so many implications when it comes to the national title race? Embarrassing. But not a total surprise.

Earlier in the week I had talked to former Georgia coach Jim Donnan, who said, "Clemson will get destroyed Saturday night. You should say that on *GameDay*." After the South Carolina incident, I decided it was best to get in and out of Clemson in one piece. So I picked Florida State to win this morning, but said it in a near-whisper, hoping the locals who already hated me wouldn't hear the prediction.

I hadn't liked Clemson's chances, but I did like LSU's odds to beat Ole Miss tonight in Oxford. In fact, I had gone out of my way to praise Lester Miles during the week.

A lot of good it did.

Whatever hopes LSU's Tigers had of working their way back into the national championship race ended tonight. They lost to the Rebels. They pulled a Clemson.

Poor Mad Hatter. He'll take some heat for a second SEC defeat. Here it is only mid-October and his team is already eliminated from the BCS Championship equation and probably from the SEC West race.

If they ever do one of those neuroimaging scans to analyze the brain function of Les Miles, I want to be there for the results.

How can you not like a guy who calls one of his daughters "Smacker"?

How can you not appreciate a guy who literally grazes on stadium grass?

How can you not cherish a guy whose press conferences are better than any Letterman or Kimmel monologue? Who rappels down twenty-four-story buildings in Baton Rouge to raise adoption awareness? What other football coach among us can pull off the "Harlem Shake"?

Miles isn't going to win a national championship this year. But in the future, he'll add to his 2007 crystal trophy. His program is too good, the recruiting base is too rich and, well, Alabama can't keep winning forever, can it?

If I could pick one coach to star in a reality series, Miles would be the choice. If I could listen to one coach's pregame or postgame locker room speech, Miles would be the easy selection. The power of his personality fascinates me.

Sometimes I have absolutely no idea what he is talking about. I don't think he knows. His mind will shut down, but his mouth keeps going. And when that happens, you get Miles mojo.

You get Miles staring down the media when rumors persist in late 2007 that he's going to return to his alma mater and become the Michigan coach. That's when he defiantly says he has an SEC Championship Game to play "and I am excited about the opportunity for my *damn* strong football team to play in it . . . Thank you very much. Have a great day."

You get Miles explaining how eating blades of stadium grass "humbles me as a man [and] lets me know I'm a part of the field and part of the game . . . I'll tell you one thing—the grass at Tiger Stadium tastes best."

You get Miles praising his team after a 2012 comeback against Ole Miss, telling reporters that his players are "a spectacular group of men. You go find them, you throw your arms around them, you give them a big kiss on the mouth—if you're a girl. Wow, what a game! Huh?!"

You get Miles reminding us earlier in the week that Columbus Day has arrived. "All those of you that know Italians, like Italians, or the people that might venture onto a ship and travel to explore and find new lands, this is your day. It's not St. Paddy's Day. That's a different day entirely."

And Miles is a different kind of coach entirely.

In May 2012 I was the emcee of a charity event in Birmingham. This was just four months after then–No. 1 LSU had lost to Bama in the BCS Championship, and only a few months before the Tigers would be ranked as the 2012 preseason No. 1 in *USA Today*'s coaches poll. Miles was the featured speaker for the event.

I stood in front of the large audience and said, "Our guest speaker is one of the greatest coaches and most influential men in the game today. Not only is he a remarkable leader, his accomplishments are vast both on and off the field. Respected across the nation for his innovation and leadership, our guest speaker has soared to the top of his profession. With three national championships and the universal support and adoration of a large fan base, our guest—

"Oops, I'm sorry. I mistakenly picked up tomorrow's Rotary Club introduction of Nick Saban."

For the record, Miles howled at the introduction.

But Miles could give it back. Shortly after I was hired at ESPN, I moderated an on-air panel discussion with Miles, Richt and Sumlin during the SEC coaches' car wash. "Car wash" is the term they use at ESPN to describe how visiting coaches and players make the rounds—from ESPN TV show to TV show, from radio show to radio show, to podcast, to ESPN.com interviews.

The panel discussion took place the same week that I had been critical of Sumlin's handling of Manziel. I had been known to criticize Richt, and I had a reputation for being sympathetic to Alabama. So I wasn't exactly a popular guy with these three coaches.

As we waited to tape the segment for *College Football Live*, it was hard not to feel the awkwardness and tension in the room. That's when Miles had said something like, "Paul, I can't believe you don't have your Crimson Tide shirt on."

Great. The last thing I needed was for Miles to say something like that when the red light came on.

"Coach, it's only my entire career on the line here," I told him. "So can you give me a break?"

To his credit, Miles didn't say anything about me and Bama. But I'm sure he loved making me squirm.

People make the mistake of underestimating Miles. They watch him bluster on TV and they think he's a cartoon character. They listen to his non sequiturs and dismiss him as a goofball.

I probably made that mistake early on. He had a couple of rocky years, by LSU standards, in 2008 and 2009, and I wondered if he could survive the hot seat. Survive it? Miles feeds off that kind of pressure. He was back to double-digit wins in 2010 and in the BCS Championship Game in 2011.

Saban doesn't think he's a goofball. OK, maybe a little bit, if only because their personalities are so different. But Saban has lost games to Miles at home and on the road. He lost games to Miles in 2010 and 2011. He knows what Miles can do at LSU because it was Saban's LSU program that Miles inherited in 2005.

Saban doesn't scare Miles. That's what makes the Bama-LSU rivalry so much fun. Miles doesn't back down to anyone.

Remember how he coached against Saban in the 2012 game? Miles tried a fake field goal. It didn't work. He tried an onside kick. It didn't work. He went for it on fourth down. It didn't work. LSU lost the game, but it wasn't from lack of trying.

Even at three and a half years old, I appear skeptical about the whole Santa thing. My sister Pam, less so.

(Courtesy of the Finebaum family)

Ah, the good ol' days: when I actually needed a brush to comb my hair.

(Courtesy of the Finebaum family)

A bet is a bet. I said if Auburn beat Alabama in 1989, I'd ride a tractor to the Loveliest Village on the Plains. Auburn won, so Farmer Paul got on his tractor.

(Courtesy of the Finebaum family)

Little-known fact: Harrison Ford patterned his Indiana Jones character after me. At least, that's what I tell people.

(Francie Hogan)

The eternally cheerful "Robert from Waterloo" is one of my favorite callers. When Robert Fisher invited me to his home in Iowa to talk football, I couldn't refuse.

(Rick Chase/Waterloo Courier)

Musician . . . War Eagle. No show is complete without a call from I-Man.

(Courtesy of I-Man)

The Legendary Legend. My only caller who claims he spent time in the Big House (and I don't mean Michigan Stadium) for a capital crime.

(Courtesy of Ben Flanagan/Al.com)

Phyllis from Mulga is so pro-Bama that she wants to be buried in a houndstooth coffin. The only caller to appeal and overturn a lifetime ban from the show.

(Courtesy of Phyllis from Mulga)

The most infamous fan in college football history, Harvey Updyke, poisoner of Toomer's Corner. And to think, I almost hung up the phone in the middle of his confession call.

(Mugshots.com)

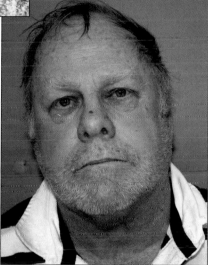

What can I say? Another satisfied Finebaum listener.

On the set during our College *GameDay* visit to USC. (*Left to right:* David Pollack, me, Desmond Howard, Chris Fowler, Lee Corso and Kirk Herbstreit). For once, Desmond isn't yelling at me.

(ESPN Images)

The day an Alabama recruiter told Bo Jackson he'd have to sit the bench his freshman year was the day Bo decided on Auburn.

(Courtesy of Auburn University)

Herschel Walker and the Heisman Trophy were made for each other. Check out that UGA sportcoat.

(Courtesy of the University of Georgia)

Before he was Broadway Joe, he was Alabama's Joe Namath. Bear Bryant called him the greatest athlete he ever coached. They won a national championship together in 1964.

(Courtesy of the University of Alabama)

The legend: Bear Bryant and his houndstooth hat. During my newspaper days, I had a private phone audience with him once a week.

(Courtesy of the University of Alabama)

Say hello to Johnny Manziel, the most electrifying, polarizing and news-making quarterback in decades. It took me a while, but Johnny Football won me over.

(Glen Johnson/Texas A&M)

If Tim Tebow isn't the greatest quarterback in college football history, he's on the shortest of short lists.

(David Bergman/Corbis)

Peyton Manning never won a national championship at Tennessee, but he should have won the Heisman Trophy in 1997.

(Courtesy of the University of Tennessee)

Nobody could stop Auburn's Cam Newton in 2010. Not Alabama in the Iron Bowl. Not Oregon in the BCS Championship. Not the NCAA.

(Courtesy of Auburn University)

The second-best coach in the country (behind Nick Saban): Ohio State's Urban Meyer. One day Florida fans will forgive him for leaving (OK, maybe not).

(Courtesy of Ohio State University)

The eccentric Les Miles of LSU. How can you not love a coach who wins national championships and likes eating stadium grass?

(Courtesy of LSU Sports Information)

Auburn's Gus Malzahn always dreamed of turning college football upside down with his offense. He has Bama's attention.

(Courtesy of Auburn University)

Clip and save photo: Bama coach Nick Saban . . . smiling! You'd smile, too, if AJ McCarron was your quarterback and you'd won three BCS Championships in four years.

(Courtesy of the University of Alabama)

In many ways, what Steve Spurrier has done at South Carolina is more impressive than what he did at Florida. The Head Ball Coach and his visor energized the SEC.

(Associated Press)

Auburn's Chris Davis returns Bama's missed field goal attempt 109 yards for the winning Iron Bowl score. Quite simply, the greatest ending in the greatest college football game.

(Courtesy of Auburn University)

Crimson Tide kicker Cade Foster deserved better than Iron Bowl scapegoat status. There was plenty of blame to go around in Kick Bama Kick.

(John David Merker/USA Today Sports)

A streak that will likely never be broken: seven seasons (2006–2012), seven consecutive national championships by SEC teams. *(Top row)* Nick Saban and Alabama. *(Middle row)* LSU's Les Miles and Saban. *(Bottom row)* Auburn's Gene Chizik and Florida's Urban Meyer, twice.

(Photos are courtesy of LSU Sports Information, the University of Alabama, Associated Press, and Mike Blake/Reuters/Corbis)

When the Michigan job came open at the end of the 2007 season, I thought he might leave. When it came open at the end of the 2010, I was surprised he didn't. I thought the lure of Ann Arbor would convince him to return to Michigan, where he had lettered as an offensive lineman and later coached under Bo Schembechler. I don't think it's a better job, but it is much easier to win a conference championship in the Big Ten than in the SEC.

Ah, but LSU is a very intoxicating place—and I'm not talking about the alcohol that flows so freely there on a Saturday night. Miles likes LSU. His family likes it. But more than anything, Miles can win there.

Michigan is a stuffed-shirt kind of place. It takes itself much too seriously. *Michigan Men* and all that. Get over yourself.

Miles isn't a stuffed-shirt kind of guy. He might have been born and raised in Ohio, but the football soul of Les Miles is all Louisiana.

I think you woke up this morning, scratched the chicken out of your eyes and said, "I'm going to provoke the HELL out of some Alabama fans today." Oh, my goodness, Paul. I am so mad at you right now.

—SPARROW FROM HUNTSVILLE

CHAPTER 12

Masters of the Universe

Sunday, October 27, 2013
Charlotte, North Carolina

THE SEASON SKINNY: Nos. 1 and 2 keep winning big–Bama over Tennessee, Florida State over North Carolina State. . . . Missouri's unbeaten season ends in a double-overtime home loss to South Carolina. . . . Days after the NCAA *finally* rules on the nearly four-year-old Miami infractions case (no new bowl bans, nine scholarship reductions), the Hurricanes celebrate with a comeback win against Wake Forest.

There are lots of SEC haters in the world. But if they would take a moment to rest their squirrel-sized brains, they'd realize that the SEC basically invented the version of college football we enjoy today. In fact, every other conference, from the Pac-12 to the MAC, should send a thank-you note and a basket of fine meats and cheeses to the SEC offices in Birmingham. While we're at it, everybody connected with college football should send a modest cash gift to the SEC.

Almost every conference in the country copied the SEC's league championship game. Almost every conference copied the SEC's expansion template. Almost every conference tried to copy the SEC's stadium and facilities arms race. The only thing those other conferences can't copy is the SEC's passion for football and the decibel level it creates. Or as sports columnist Chuck Culpepper once wrote of the SEC: " . . . they'd spun a noise . . . with peer only in the soccer theaters of Europe and South America."

In other words, loud, and getting louder all the time.

In the late 1980s, I sat in the office of SEC commissioner Harvey Schiller and listened with skepticism as the former Air Force brigadier general detailed his vision for a new SEC. Schiller had earned his undergraduate degree at The Citadel, flown combat missions during the Vietnam War (earning the Distinguished Flying Cross) and taught chemistry at the Air Force Academy. His office reflected those military sensibilities. It was sparsely decorated (a framed photo of the Academy's Colorado Springs campus is the only item I remember hanging on the wall), orderly, functional and clean. It wasn't meant to be comfortable; it was meant to be a place where serious business was conducted.

Schiller outlined, in a matter-of-fact tone, an expansion plan to add more member schools (mighty Texas was on his list of possibilities). He proposed a conference championship game. He said he envisioned a time when the SEC would expand its television footprint from regional to national. He spoke of sponsorship deals. And the more he talked, the more I thought Harvey Schiller was an enigmatic dreamer whose ideas were doomed to failure.

Expansion? Championship games? The SEC a TV darling? Corporate sponsors? Who was he kidding?

I didn't believe any of it was possible back then. The SEC was almost a mom-and-pop entity. It moved slowly. It embraced change slowly. What Schiller was proposing was futuristic, almost inconceivable for the SEC. He had interesting concepts, but never did I think he would gain enough support within the conference to make the ideas a reality.

Schiller was proposing nothing less than a revolution in college football. He saw the future and he wanted the SEC to be part of it. Too bad he didn't stick around to see it happen.

Schiller left the SEC for the USOC in late 1989, just before the revolution began. In this year's SEC media guide, on the pages that detail the conference's historical time line, Schiller's tenure receives exactly

twenty-one words. That's a shame, because Schiller had a genius quality to him that will never be appreciated by those who consider him an
SEC footnote, or by those who stupidly don't consider him at all. But
the SEC wouldn't be the SEC without him.

If Schiller laid the foundation of the modern SEC, Roy Kramer
built the house. It was Kramer who took advantage of an NCAA loop-
hole (first discovered by Schiller) that allowed a twelve-team conference
to split into divisions and hold a conference championship. Nobody saw
that coming.

To be fair, the SEC wasn't the first conference to expand. Georgia
Tech had joined the ACC in 1978, the same year the University of Arizona and Arizona State University turned the Pac-8 into the Pac-10.
Soon, in 1989, the Big Ten would invite then-independent Penn State to
join its conference, giving that league eleven members.

Arkansas and South Carolina joined the SEC in 1990 (after FSU
got cold feet and the Texas legislature put the kibosh on the Longhorns
leaving the Southwest Conference) and began play in 1992.

It was Kramer who convinced the SEC school presidents to approve
an SEC Championship Game, which also made its debut in 1992. Bama
beat Florida at Birmingham's Legion Field, and about four weeks later,
the Tide defeated Miami in the Sugar Bowl for the national championship. The other conference commissioners couldn't help but notice the
sold-out Legion Field crowd of 83,091 (*cha-ching*) and the 9.8 rating it
drew on ABC's national telecast. Excluding the BCS National Championship, the ratings for that 1992 game were higher than the ratings
of each of the four BCS bowls (Sugar, Orange, Rose and Fiesta) in the
2012 season.

It was Kramer who pushed to move the game to Atlanta after two
years in Birmingham. At the time, I was a vocal opponent of the move.
I thought it was a sneaky decision and disrespectful of a city that had
helped clear and provide the land for the new SEC offices, and given

the conference a sweetheart property rental deal. Birmingham had been there for the SEC when the league had needed it most.

Kramer argued that Birmingham and Legion Field didn't have a big-city, big-stadium feel to it. The $214 million Georgia Dome had opened in 1992, and Kramer saw it as the perfect host for the conference championship.

He was right, I was wrong. It turned out to be one of the great decisions in SEC history.

I remember walking out of the Georgia Dome after No. 6–ranked Florida beat No. 3–ranked Alabama by a single point in 1994 and thinking, "Wow, this place is pretty cool." Suddenly, Legion Field seemed very old, like it needed one of those aluminum walkers with tennis balls on the bottom of the legs. That first-ever SEC Championship at the Dome gave ABC its highest-rated college football game since 1991.

It was also Kramer, the former Central Michigan head coach and Vanderbilt athletic director, who negotiated contracts with ABC and Jefferson Pilot Sports in 1992. Later he pulled CBS, ESPN and assorted bowl games under the widening SEC roof.

But when it comes to the SEC's ultimate transformation into the towering Cyclops of college football, Mike Slive rightfully deserves the credit. Slive traded his commissionership of Conference USA for the SEC in 2002, which is like trading your Prius for a Tesla full of the best eighteen-year-old athletes in the country.

Slive is basically your grandfather: thoughtful, kind and soft. But I've seen Slive's other side, the side that you would be wise to avoid at all costs.

He has degrees from Dartmouth, Virginia and Georgetown. The son of Russian immigrants, he is a former judge and a former lawyer, and was an athletic director in the Ivy League and an assistant executive director in the Pac-10. He has served as the BCS coordinator, as the Division I men's basketball selection committee chairman, and as chairman of the NCAA Infractions Appeals Committee. The man's been around.

I didn't think Slive would last a year in the SEC. I thought he would feel like an interloper, too worldly for the South. I knew him a little bit from his days at C-USA. When I heard he would replace Kramer, it seemed like a peculiar match, like chocolate syrup on tuna fish.

I had been conditioned during the Kramer Era to think the next SEC commissioner should and would have some sort of playing/coaching background. And certainly nobody was going to confuse Slive's C-USA with big-time football. Were his teams even *on* TV?

What I couldn't see for myself was that instead of a former coach, the SEC needed a good lawyer, especially a lawyer who had founded a firm that specialized in representing schools with NCAA troubles. And few conferences had more NCAA troubles than the SEC.

In July 2002, half the schools in the SEC were either on NCAA probation or under NCAA investigation. There was a twenty-five-year period, extending into the late 2000s, during which at least one SEC school was on NCAA probation.

Me and everybody else who gave a damn about the SEC rolled our eyes when Slive said in 2003 that his goal was to be probation-free in five years.

I actually told Slive at the time, "Commissioner, you don't know what you're getting into there."

Slive didn't care. The important thing was to articulate the position. I don't know if he truly believed he could clean up the conference, but he wanted his coaches and athletic directors to know he was going to try. The SEC has had its share of major NCAA violations during his tenure, but not anywhere near the same level of lawlessness as before.

Slive signed new long-term deals with CBS and ESPN in 2008. It was a smart play at the time because the SEC wasn't prepared to do what the Big Ten had done in 2006: launch its own network. I don't think it could have supported it. The value wasn't there yet. And I'm not sure Slive wanted to spend the money it would take to create the network from scratch.

Of course, it would be ridiculous to ignore the role that integration played in the SEC's rise to power (thank you, Nat Northington and others). Had the SEC not been pulled kicking and screaming into the twentieth century, it would now be college football's version of the world's tallest midget.

Slive has quietly pushed SEC presidents and athletic directors to hire more minority coaches. His fingerprints could be found on the Sylvester Croom hiring at Mississippi State. And I know he took great pride in the events of November 12, 2011. That's when, for the first time in SEC history, two African-American coaches faced each other in a game: James Franklin of Vanderbilt and Joker Phillips of Kentucky.

And who knows—maybe one day the SEC will have an African-American commissioner.

I could never be commissioner of the SEC. First of all, nobody is ever going to ask me. And if they did, I'd say no. You have to be nice to too many people.

But if I *were* SEC commissioner for a day, I would never dare touch the Iron Bowl. However, I would move Auburn to the SEC East and Missouri to the SEC West. I mean, seriously—Missouri borders Nebraska and it plays in the same SEC division as Florida? Dumb.

Instead of playing commissioner, I'd rather play the Mount Rushmore game: Who are the four rock bands that belong on the side of a mountain? What are the four movies? Who are the four actors? Give me enough time and I can come up with all sorts of Mount Rushmore foursomes.

But how do you limit it to four when picking the seminal figures in SEC football history?

I've got it: Bear Bryant, Bo Jackson, Herschel Walker, Kramer.

No, wait: Bryant, Slive, Saban and Bo.

Wait: Robert Neyland, Bryant, Saban and Spurrier.

One more try: Bryant, Spurrier, Saban and Slive.

You know what? I give up.

I don't always watch football, but when I do, I arbitrarily
rank inferior teams in front of FSU. Because bias.

—SIGN AT FLORIDA STATE WITH PHOTO OF ME AS THE MOST
INTERESTING MAN IN THE WORLD

CHAPTER 13

A Small Rant

Saturday, November 2, 2013
Tallahassee, Florida

THE SEASON SKINNY: Auburn defeats Arkansas at Fayetteville, dropping the Razorbacks to 0-5 in the SEC and ending a week in which Razorbacks coach Bret Bielema accused the Tigers staff of gamesmanship by not sending complete game videos. . . . So much for ACC balance–Florida State beats Miami, 41–14, meaning the Seminoles have beaten the Hurricanes and Clemson by a combined score of 92–28. . . . Alabama and Oregon are No. 1 and 2 in the BCS Standings. . . . FSU's Winston is putting up better numbers in key metrics than Manziel did in 2012.

If the season ended tonight, Alabama would play Florida State in the BCS Championship. That is according to the latest projections for Sunday's BCS Standings.

If the season ended tonight, there also would be riots in the streets of Eugene, Oregon, and Columbus, Ohio, and Waco, Texas.

Five teams (Bama, FSU, Oregon, Ohio State and Baylor) are still undefeated. Each one thinks it could reach the national title game. I've quit trying to figure out the polls, the BCS Standings and the BCS computers. That's why ESPN's Brad Edwards was put on Earth, to figure it out for me.

I've also quit trying to figure out this concept of "SEC fatigue." Everybody is using the term these days as if it were a medical discovery.

You hear a lot about SEC fatigue from fans in non-SEC conferences. You hear it from certain media members who cover certain other conferences. What they ought to call it is "Big Ten fatigue." "Pac-12 fatigue." "ACC fatigue." "Big 12 fatigue." Those conferences are tired. They're tired of watching the SEC win national title after national title.

Citing SEC fatigue is just another way of saying, "We can't beat you." It's an excuse. It's a manufactured reason for failure.

The concept of SEC fatigue met its birth mother in 2011. That's when LSU beat Alabama in overtime at Tuscaloosa, 9–6. It knocked Bama out of the national championship race.

That is, until it got right back in.

Thanks to assorted upsets, the Tide worked its way into the No. 2 spot of the final BCS Standings. It played No. 1 LSU in New Orleans and won, 21–0.

The game was as interesting as an afternoon of C-SPAN. But how is that the SEC's fault? The two best teams in the country played in that game. End of debate.

Bama would have steamrolled any team you put out there that night. Ever since then, the backlash against the SEC (and the accusations that it somehow gamed the BCS system) has grown. In fact, some folks have held a grudge against the SEC since the mid-1990s, when then–SEC commissioner Roy Kramer pushed so hard for the BCS to replace the Bowl Alliance in 1998. Once that happened, it wasn't long before SEC teams (Tennessee was the first) started winning BCS Championships. Conspiracy theories abounded, the most popular being that Kramer worked behind the scenes to somehow influence poll voting, or that he favored certain computer polls because their metrics would rate SEC teams higher in their rankings. An SEC plot to rule the world!

None of it was true. Kramer preferred that SEC teams win the national championship, but nobody, including Kramer, could manip-ulate an entire system. Not with guys such as Big Ten commissioner Jim Delany looking over his shoulder. The simple truth is that Kramer cared deeply about college football and thought the BCS was the best system for the time.

Of course, if those same critics and conspiracy theorists are tired of the SEC's reign during the BCS Era, it's only going to get worse once the four-team College Football Playoff kicks off in 2014. Odds are— since the SEC can do more chin-ups than any other league—that two of the four competing teams will be Alabama, Auburn, LSU, Georgia, Florida or Ole Miss.

Had there been a playoff in 2012, Florida might have reached the final four. Or perhaps the selection committee would have done the right thing and rewarded Georgia for beating the Gators during the regular season and nearly beating defending national champion Bama in the SEC title game. There were already two SEC teams in the 2011 title game. Alabama would have reached a make-believe four-team playoff in 2008.

So when it comes to future football final four scenarios, the SEC isn't fatigued at all. It's just getting started.

That's what makes me so mad about Paul Finebaum.
He loves Alabama. He'll say he don't, but he does. He makes
me sick. He's a loser. Whatever.

—TAMMY

CHAPTER 14

Saint Nick

Saturday, November 9, 2013

Tuscaloosa, Alabama

THE SEASON SKINNY: A Condi Rice aide confirms that Penn State approached the former secretary of state about becoming the school's president. She isn't interested. . . . A Texas big-money booster tells the *Dallas Morning News* that newly named Texas Longhorns athletic director Steve Patterson has "other issues" than worrying about Mack Brown's future. . . . Oregon's BCS hopes take a hit after loss at Stanford.

At exactly 6:39 a.m. local time, I leave the recruiting room inside the north end zone facility at Bryant-Denny Stadium and make the short trip to the *GameDay* set, located in the same Walk of Champions area as the statues of Bama's national championship football coaches: Nick Saban, Bear Bryant, Frank Thomas, Gene Stallings and Wallace Wade. The sun is beginning to creep up the sides of buildings. The air is cool and autumn-crisp.

It is the perfect weather for a perfect SEC rivalry: No. 13 LSU at No. 1 Bama.

This is the first time in four months that I've been in Tuscaloosa. It is a homecoming of sorts for me. I haven't spent much time in the state—and even less in Tuscaloosa—since the radio show moved to the ESPN studios in Charlotte. I still have my home outside Birmingham and get back there on Sundays when I can, but the radio show and my travel schedule make it tough. I miss the place.

I have no idea how I'm going to be received by the Alabama faithful. My entire plan is to be low-key, to do a South Carolina and fly below the radar.

I always do an early *SportsCenter* hit before the actual *GameDay* broadcast begins. My appearance usually serves as fish chum for the show. It gets the crowd going a little bit.

I take my place on the set and glance at the growing number of Bama fans. There are signs everywhere.

"Where is Ponder?" reads one sign, referring to Samantha Ponder, who missed a recent show because she was under the weather.

There are cutout faces of Nicolas Cage, just because someone likes Nicolas Cage, I guess. There are supersized photos of a pudgy-faced David Pollack, circa University of Georgia, 2003. That's because Bama fans hold a grudge: Pollack, a *GameDay* colleague and former Bulldogs all-American defensive lineman, went 2-0 against the Tide as a player. There is something about Les Miles using Shake Weights and another sign that reads, "Les Miles Wears Crocs." (Wait, Crocs aren't cool anymore?) There is an "LSU Hates Puppies" sign. And signs mocking the Oregon Ducks (Oregon, with its "We Want Bama" T-shirts, lost to Stanford two nights earlier). There is a sign that simply says, "My Name Is Billy."

And then I notice someone waving a sign on the front row with a caricature of me on it: "Paul Finebaum . . . Coming up next on *SportsCenter*."

For reasons unknown, Queen's "Fat Bottomed Girls" plays on the loudspeakers in the promenade area. It is the first song played every Saturday on the *GameDay* set.

There are two major story lines as the game approaches:

- Will LSU end Bama's quest for the three-peat?
- Is Saban going to leave Alabama for Texas?

I answer both questions during my morning *SportsCenter* appearance. No, Alabama will not lose to LSU. In fact, I pick the Tide to win big. (Final score: Bama 38, the Hatter 17.)

And no, Saban isn't leaving Tuscaloosa for Austin. Or Austria, Australia or the Auckland Islands. He isn't leaving for anywhere.

To me, the rumors and scenarios involving Saban and Texas are part of the season's biggest nonstory. I can't believe how many members of the media perpetuate the idea of his departure. It simply doesn't make any sense.

I've heard the arguments:

The expectations at Alabama have reached toxic levels . . . No Alabama coach, not even the Bear, had to deal with such expectations . . . Texas will hand him a blank check and tell him to fill in the number.

I agree with the expectations part: Bama fans are spoiled like trust fund children. But why would Saban leave Alabama, where the expectations are absurdly high, for Texas, where the expectations are also absurdly high—and where it is more political, where Saban won't have the level of control he has at Alabama, where they have a television network dedicated entirely to all things University of Texas (which will require more of his time) and where he will have to begin another rebuilding project at age sixty two?

Answer: he won't.

More money? Saban doesn't need more money. And if he did, Alabama can afford to provide it.

The whole thing drives me nuts. Hello, will someone listen? He's . . . not . . . going . . . to . . . Texas.

The only non-Alabama coaching position I can see Saban considering is a return to the NFL, and even that seems like a long shot. He might at least listen to the offer. The NFL is Saban's last unconquered frontier. Look what happened when his good friend Bill Belichick got a second head coaching chance in the pros. The Hoodie became a legend.

Terry Saban comes by the *GameDay* bus with Nick. I ask her a question. "Terry, help me out with something. I'm really enjoying my time with *GameDay*. But if you and Nick are going to Austin, could you please let me know so I can put in my transfer to the Longhorn Network?"

She laughs, but there is a finality in her voice when she speaks about the rumors.

"We're not going to Texas," she says.

Let's face it: the Sabans are the First Couple of the state of Alabama. First of all, the position itself—head football coach at Alabama—gives you a platform of power. But because of the program's wild success, Saban is the best-liked person in the state. He has the highest presence in the state. My evaluation of people's handling of power is based on whether they attempt to use it or to abuse it. Saban is very circumspect about influencing anything other than the outcome of a football game.

He's done a couple of things that have been particularly important. Symbolically, he took a leading role in the healing after sixty-two separate tornadoes, many of them lethal EF5-category twisters, swept through the state in April 2011 and left a swath of death and damage. His actions and empathy gained a lot of fans in addition to the legions he already had.

There aren't any higher-profile people in Alabama.

The next most influential man after Nick is probably accidental governor Robert Bentley, who by the way owes me his career. Before he was elected in 2010, Bentley was a semi-obscure member of the state's House of Representatives and his greatest claim to fame, at least among Bama football fans, was that he once served as the personal dermatologist to Bear Bryant.

That thin connection to Bryant was the only reason we invited Bentley on our February 16, 2010, show. When he settled into the studio guest chair that day, Bentley's campaign was barely clinging to life. According to a just-released poll, Bentley had the support of only

4 percent of the state's Republican voters. There were rumors that his campaign might not survive long enough to reach the June primary.

We spent an hour talking to him. He was very bright, which I happen to know is unusual for a candidate running for governor of Alabama.

After the appearance, Bentley's numbers pole-vaulted into instant respectability. He reached double digits in a March GOP voters poll. Campaign donations flooded in. He eventually won the general election by a landslide. When people ask him about me, he says, "That's the man who got me elected."

But Saban is Nos. 1 through 10 on the list of Alabama power brokers. He would be in the top ten even without having won three national titles at Bama.

Saban has the most visible job in the state, and given the religiosity with which Alabamans apply themselves to college football, he has become the pontiff of pigskin. He's definitely the most powerful coach in the sport and, according to *USA Today*, the highest paid.

I think his age helps. He's not a thirty-five-year-old coach who has emerged from the pack and is always looking to take the next step up the ladder. In the college game, Saban is standing atop the ladder. He's run out of rungs to climb. The truth is, it's easier to scale the summit than to stay there. That's the real brilliance of Saban—he's managed to stay near or at the top of the college game for almost a dozen years.

People forget the dismal state of the Bama program when Shula was fired after the 2006 regular season. Morale was low. Wins were hard to come by. Bama couldn't afford another hiring mistake, not after the conga line of failed and flawed coaches such as DuBose, Franchione, Price and Shula.

Mal Moore was in a difficult position. His football program had been devalued by the coaching turnover and NCAA sanctions (a five-year probation beginning in 2002, along with a two-year bowl ban and a three-year reduction in scholarship numbers). But as they say in the real estate business about houses, Bama football had "good bones." It was a fix-me-upper mansion.

Saban and Spurrier were the initial targets. But Spurrier didn't want to leave South Carolina after just two years. Saban, meanwhile, was trying to figure out a way to squeeze his Miami Dolphins into the NFL playoffs. Alabama was a distraction, and Saban hates distractions. So he began deflecting Bama-related questions and kept assuring Dolphins owner Wayne Huizenga that he was staying put.

So Saban was out of the mix—or so we thought. That meant Alabama had been turned down by its two leading candidates.

Plan C was then–West Virginia coach Rich Rodriguez. Bama officials interviewed Rodriguez in New York during the National Football Foundation Hall of Fame festivities. He accepted the job on a Thursday and the introductory press conference was scheduled for Friday in Tuscaloosa.

But Rodriguez backed out of the deal when the governor of West Virginia, Joe Manchin (now the state's U.S. senator and a longtime friend of Saban's), helped broker a last-minute contract to keep the coach where he was. The story broke as our show was about to start at two p.m.

When I came on the air and said, "Rich Rodriguez has turned down Alabama," you could almost hear a collective gasp across the state. Moore was speechless. So were Alabama fans. They couldn't comprehend that the coach of a West Virginia program that had never won a national championship (and had come close only once) had said yes and then no to mighty Bama. It was one of the darkest days in Alabama football history.

For a brief period during the show, callers accused me of sabotaging the Bama romance with Rodriguez. The callers had been fueled by a Mobile radio station host who had suggested I had somehow made fun of Rita Rodriguez, the coach's wife, earlier in the week. Then the message boards got involved and suddenly I was to blame for Rich Rod staying put.

It wasn't true, of course. In retrospect, I wish it had been; I'd be a hero in Tuscaloosa.

A year after turning down Bama—and only four months after he signed a contract extension with West Virginia—Rodriguez took the Michigan job. He was 15-22 at Michigan (6-18 against Big Ten competition, 0-6 vs. Ohio State and Michigan State, 0-12 vs. teams that finished the season ranked) and suffered the worst bowl loss in Michigan history (a 38-point defeat to SEC member Mississippi State). It was during Rodriguez's failed three-year stay at Michigan that the football program was found guilty of multiple major NCAA rules violations (a first for the proud U-M program), put on probation and compelled to self-impose a series of sanctions.

Yeah, so I feel terrible about "costing" Bama its chance at Rich Rodriguez. I'll take full responsibility for Rich Rod's not coming to Tuscaloosa. And while we're at it, I'll also take responsibility for Saban's accepting the job.

I mean, why let the facts get in the way of a great story, right?

It was one of the wildest days in my career. I had to rewrite my newspaper column as I was doing the radio show. And after the radio show, I had a TV gig to do.

In a typical overreaction by Bama fans, they wanted Moore fired. They were embarrassed, angry, frustrated. The program was a laughingstock.

I had made the argument that Bama needed to hire the best, and the best was Spurrier or Saban.

MSNBC's Joe Scarborough, who got his undergrad degree at Alabama and his law degree at Florida, had become something of a regular on our show and had begun campaigning for Saban. I've given him credit for this—he understood what Saban could do at a place such as Alabama. He wrote an op-ed piece in the *Birmingham News* and came on our show and said Bama needed to target Saban again and do what it needed to do to hire him.

During a December 21 press conference with local reporters, Saban was asked once again about the Bama opening. That's when he uttered the famous words, "I guess I have to say it: I'm not going to be the Alabama coach."

He had been baited into saying something, and he couldn't help himself. He got too cute for his own good.

Two weeks later, he took the Bama job.

I tried to put myself in Saban's place. I felt like if I had been in his position, and I had a football team I was responsible for, and I was trying to make the playoffs, and then somebody asked me about the Alabama job, I would have tried to mislead them, within reason. I don't mean blatantly lie. I don't think he lied. He said, "I will not be the Alabama coach."

Perhaps at that moment, he believed he wouldn't be the Bama coach. He made a serious miscalculation, but to characterize him as a liar is unfair.

There was outrage and the usual hysteria. Don Shula popped off, telling the *Miami Herald* that Saban's repeated Bama denials "tells you a bit about the guy . . . The guy likes to hear himself talk and then doesn't follow up on what he says."

Shula was mad that Bama had fired his overmatched son. The people in Miami were mad because they were getting dumped for a college team. *How dare Saban leave the Dolphins for Alabama!*

C'mon, grow up. The Dolphins haven't won a Super Bowl since Garo Yepremian was selling ties and kicking field goals. So they don't get to decide if a coach can leave them for a hallowed place like Tuscaloosa.

And by the way, Bama is by far the better job. I guarantee you Saban is making more money than Joe Philbin. I bet you he's enjoying the job more than Philbin too.

Alabama fans didn't care if Saban had misled the Dolphins. All they cared about was having a coach capable of leading the Tide to a national championship. Now they had one.

At his introductory press conference in Tuscaloosa, the visiting South Florida writers interviewed Saban in a separate room, which helped keep the presser from becoming a battle of the media agendas: the South Florida media wanting to ask about Saban's past, the Alabama media wanting to ask him about the Crimson Tide's present and future. Saban addressed his Miami comments and tried to move on. But the national media didn't want to move on. They said he couldn't be trusted, that he'd surely leave Alabama at the first opportunity.

Guess what? He's still there.

I took a very strong position defending him. I knew that if he was successful at Bama, the Tide faithful would have his back. And that's exactly what has happened.

The incident—or, more correctly, the reaction to his Miami denial—hurt him deeply. I think it still bothers him.

They'd never admit it, but Saban intimidates most of the coaches he faces. He's already ahead by a touchdown, maybe two, before kickoff. Nine times out of ten, he has the better schemes, the better staff and the better players.

In short, he's Nick Saban and Joe Philbin isn't.

Here's how you know other SEC coaches are in desperation mode when it comes to Saban: At a January 2013 high school sports banquet in Macon, Georgia, Vanderbilt's James Franklin told the audience, "There's this guy at Alabama. I think his name is Nicky Satan. I think you guys have probably heard of him before. I'm going to outwork him, and that's kind of our plan every single day."

Nobody is going to outwork Saban. It isn't possible. Bryant couldn't have outworked Saban. Franklin won't. The Mercedes-Benz assembly plant in Vance, Alabama, would have a hard time keeping up with the guy.

Saban has the best system. He has the best approach. He is the most single-minded, determined coach I've ever met. When you win a national title, your ability to get the best players increases. Five-star recruits like seeing themselves wearing championship rings and love programs that have a pipeline to the NFL.

If you're an opposing coach, Saban is your worst nightmare. He is a CEO who coaches as if he's a grad assistant trying to get a full-time job. He is a fanatic when it comes to attention to detail. And he is always looking ahead.

The week after Alabama beat Texas for the 2009 national championship (the Tide's first title in nearly twenty years), I saw Saban at a cocktail party in Houston honoring him as the Bear Bryant Coach of the Year.

I walked up to him and said, "Coach, congratulations on winning the championship. You must be very gratified."

"I don't know," he said, exhaling as if the whole thing was a major inconvenience. "You win, but with every championship you've got a new set of problems and issues."

That is quintessential Saban: a joyless winner. He's the kind of guy who would greet a winning lottery ticket with, "How much is this going to cost me in taxes?" He once told me that as great as it was to reach a BCS Championship, "It really sets your recruiting schedule back an entire week."

Saban says he has a twenty-four-hour rule: you can celebrate a victory or wallow in defeat for twenty-four hours—no more. But with him, I think it's more like twenty-four seconds. I walked away from our brief conversation that night in Houston thinking, "Are you kidding me?"

I did make him laugh once.

Well, not laugh, but smile.

In the spring of 2012, my wife and I visited Washington, D.C. I had pulled one of the very few strings I have and got us a private West Wing tour. (A friend of mine who is a former U.S. attorney was buddies with Vice President Joe Biden and, well . . .) We pulled up to the White House on a Friday night in a Yellow Cab and tried not to look like eight-year-olds going to Disney World for the first time. But we couldn't help it.

As we went through security, a nearby guard said, "You're Paul Finebaum!" He was from Pelham, Alabama, and had listened to my show over the years. We were in.

It was a great tour. We were able to do everything except veto a bill. We even saw President Obama—not in person, but there was a huge photo of him on the hallway wall leading from near the Oval Office to the Rose Garden. And posing in the photo with the world's most powerful man was the world's most powerful college football coach: Saban.

Fast-forward to New York, December 2012. I saw Saban after an awards dinner and said, "I happened to be at the White House not long ago, and was strolling around and there you were, on the wall with Obama."

"Really?" he said.

And that's when it happened: he smiled.

He was pretty proud that he and his Alabama program were featured on that White House wall with the president. Can't say that I blame him.

Saban isn't Bryant, nor does he try to be. That's smart. And no, Saban wasn't born in Alabama. But who cares? Bryant was born in Arkansas. Knute Rockne, the Bear Bryant of Notre Dame, was born in Norway. General Robert Neyland, the Bryant of Tennessee, was born in Texas. LSU's Les Miles, who is in his own Mad Hatter orbit, was born in Ohio. Saban was born in West Virginia.

He is his own man. Bama's football sensibilities have changed because of him, not the other way around.

It's unfair to put it this way, but Saban has created such a machine at Alabama that when you look at any given regular-season schedule in any Saban-coached year you say, "OK, there are nine wins there before the first game is played." Then there are three remaining games (maybe an early nonconference power opponent, Texas A&M with Manziel, LSU or Auburn) that aren't stone-cold locks.

Again, these are unfair expectations, but they are also the ultimate testament and compliment to Saban's coaching, recruiting and organizational abilities. Some coaches make us believe anything is possible. Saban makes us believe anything is probable.

Saban must drive his staff nuts. Everything has to be just so. On the first day of practice, the legendary UCLA basketball coach John Wooden used to teach his players the proper way to put on their socks and tie their shoes (two pairs of socks, the shoes a half size small). If they did it his way, they had a better chance of not getting blisters on their feet. No blisters meant more practice time. More practice time meant more potential game time. There was always a reason behind the seemingly most ordinary decisions.

Saban is the same way.

He has those four national championships, but it could have been six by now. His Bama teams in 2008 and 2010 were more than capable of winning national titles. I'll go to my grave knowing his 2010 team was the best team in the country, even though it lost to South Carolina and Auburn. That was the season Gamecocks quarterback Stephen Garcia had the one great game of his checkered career—and did so against Bama. It was the season of Cam Newton and the "Camback," in which the Tigers played their best when it mattered most and overcame a 24–0 second-quarter Iron Bowl deficit. You can die of old age waiting for a Saban-coached team to blow a twenty-four-point lead. I don't care if he's playing the Denver Broncos or Seattle Seahawks, it just doesn't happen.

You can argue that two of Saban's national championships—2011 and 2012—were the result of some degree of luck. Bama needed help from the football gods to reach the BCS Championship. But once the Tide got there, luck had nothing to do with it. The title victories against LSU in 2011 and Notre Dame in 2012 were thorough and complete.

You've heard Saban talk about "The Process" until you want to puncture your eardrums. And on the surface, the whole thing sounds like New Age, Tony Robbins–like hooey. But "The Process" isn't that complicated. It's efficient, just like Saban.

It says, "Do this and you'll be successful." Be purposeful, be smart, be driven and you'll put yourself in a position to win. He doesn't guarantee victories. But he's done the football math, and if you adhere to his plan, to his process, there's a good chance you'll be attending a ring ceremony soon enough.

Saban isn't a wasteful person. He doesn't talk unless he has something meaningful to say. If you sat next to him on a cross-country flight, he wouldn't tap you on the shoulder and say, "Hey, look at the pretty clouds." If he speaks to you, there's usually a message and a lesson attached to the conversation. I've never had a conversation with him when he wasn't delivering some sort of message. And the message wasn't necessarily *to* me, but *through* me. He used me, and the media in general, to communicate his messages to his players. He used us, but he did so masterfully.

Watch him at a press conference. He doesn't speak off the cuff. He has his notes, and those notes have been written long before he steps to the podium. And he has thought about those notes—about the exact wording, about the best way to deliver the meaning of those words.

Everyone says that he'll coach forever, that it's in his blood. It is in his blood, but one of these days he's going to get a transfusion. He's going to wake up and realize he's in his sixties, he's accomplished a great deal and maybe it's time to kick back and enjoy a rose or two.

I asked Spurrier once, "Why'd you leave Florida for the Redskins?" He said, "Well, we had just won the Orange Bowl, finished number three in the country, and all people talked about was that we had the best team and we should have won it all."

Spurrier had come face-to-face with the coaching law of diminishing returns. He had created a beast and the beast had to be fed each season. A major bowl victory was met with yawns. A ten-win season was considered a failure. A No. 3 ranking was a disappointment.

So Spurrier left. And Saban will reach a point where it will all become too much. The joy of the chase will be outweighed by the misery of the expectations.

Saban doesn't coach for the money, the fame or the statues. I'm sure he's a little embarrassed that there's a statue of him outside Bryant-Denny Stadium. Saban isn't a statue kind of guy. He's the son of a blue-collar West Virginian.

He isn't chasing Bear Bryant's shadow, or the Bear's six national titles (seven, if you want to count 1950, when his Kentucky team beat the already crowned No. 1 Oklahoma in the Sugar Bowl). Saban is secure enough in his own skin and with his own legacy to walk away from the game and not think twice about Bryant's records.

Right now, Saban is chasing whatever ideal and goal he has set for himself. I don't think it's a number, but a standard. It's like Muschamp said back in July at the SEC Media Days when he observed that Saban was in legacy-building mode.

There are Bama and non-Bama fans who think Bryant was the greatest coach in the history of coaches. They think he was responsible for everything from spearheading the South's resurgence to teaching John Travolta how to dance in *Saturday Night Fever.*

If I had to rank the coaches, would I put Saban ahead of Bryant? Bryant has two more national championships, but Saban coaches in a football world far more competitive, complex and difficult than the world Bryant's teams dominated.

When Bryant coached, you could win a national title without playing a bowl game against one of the top-five-ranked teams in the country (it happened twice to Bama and Bryant).

You could *lose* a bowl game (it happened twice to Bama and Bryant) and still end the season as No. 1.

Saban's four national championships have come against BCS No. 1 Oklahoma, No. 2 Texas, No. 1 LSU and No. 1 (cough, cough) Notre Dame.

Bryant's Bama teams played twelve games max, including a bowl. Saban's Bama teams have played as many as fourteen games in a season three different times.

Bryant had more scholarships to work with. He never had to play Auburn at Auburn. He never had to survive an SEC Championship Game.

Saban has fewer wins and fewer national titles than Bryant. But if I had to pick one coach to win me one game, I'd take Saban. And if I had to rank them right now, I'd give Saban the slightest edge.

And now if you'll excuse me, I have to go seek police protection.

This might sound like a hedge, but I'm not saying Saban is necessarily a better coach. After all, the Bear was a master at adapting to the football times. He would have been successful in any era, including this one.

But I think Saban's accomplishments have been achieved under more difficult circumstances than those faced by Bryant.

Bryant loyalists are going to think I'm crazy. They're going to want to strangle me with houndstooth-decorated piano wire.

If you think Bryant is still the greatest college coach in football history, that's fine. But the width and breadth of Saban's accomplishments have forced the issue and created the argument.

You take the Bear. I'll take The Process.

When Bama hired Saban, I said he'd win a national championship within four years. I was ridiculed for the prediction.

Well, I was wrong. He won one within three years.

Saban came on our show the very first day he was hired. It was the only show he did. People would call in and ask me, "You hated Perkins, Curry, Shula and Franchione, but you like Saban. Why?"

That's easy: he wins. He is no-nonsense and he doesn't care about inconsequential things, such as radio hosts.

I've been to Saban's house, but I'm realistic about our relationship. If I died tomorrow, he *might* send flowers to my wife. But I don't think he'd cut short a recruiting visit to be there for the funeral.

Paul and that show . . . it's let people know Alabama is not a bunch of corn-eating, inbred hooligans running around with half their clothes on, with no teeth. I get on the phone and say, "Look, I have teeth." I just think Paul Finebaum picked the state that was hurting the most, that was humiliated the most, and that was heartbroken the most. It gave them a voice to get on the radio.

—PHYLLIS FROM MULGA

The Prayer

Saturday, November 16, 2013

Los Angeles, California

THE SEASON SKINNY: According to reports, Florida State's Jameis Winston is being investigated in connection with a sexual assault complaint filed in December 2012. Winston's attorney says his client is innocent of any criminal wrongdoing (and says he has two witnesses to prove it), while the state attorney general criticizes the Tallahassee Police Department for its handling of the case. Suddenly Winston has much bigger concerns than the Heisman race. . . . Five SEC teams are in the top eleven of the BCS Standings. . . . Fresh off an upset against Oregon, Stanford loses on the road to USC. . . . Oddsmaker Danny Sheridan has Alabama as a 17-point favorite over Auburn, and a 5-point favorite against FSU in the BCS Championship.

This can't be happening. Auburn can't be on the verge of ruining an Iron Bowl matchup for the ages, can it? Auburn has blown a 20-point fourth-quarter lead! I can't believe it. Three touchdowns in less than eight minutes. From the bar of the USAir lounge I look at my watch: I've got less than thirty minutes until my connection to Birmingham. In fact, the departures monitor says the flight is beginning to board. But I can't leave. Not yet.

I had caught a flight out of Los Angeles not long after Coach Corso had bloodied himself while waving a USC sword during his *GameDay* headgear pick. He had taken the upset, going with the home Trojans over No. 4 Stanford. Coach had never lost when picking USC (and he wouldn't lose this time, either). Now I'm sitting in Charlotte chewing my fingernails off as No. 25 Georgia takes a 38–37 lead against No. 7 Auburn with 1:49 left to play.

With apologies to Stanford and USC, only two games interest me today: No. 1 Alabama at Mississippi State and this one. As always, I'm rooting for the best story, and the best story is an upcoming Iron Bowl that features an undefeated Bama against a once-beaten Auburn. The last thing the Iron Bowl needs is for the Bulldogs (the ones from Starkville and Athens) to screw things up with a pair of Saturday upsets.

During the flight from L.A., I kept checking on the UGA-Auburn score. Auburn was ahead by 20 points late in the second quarter. That's not the same thing as being ahead by 20 late in the fourth quarter, but I figured Auburn would be OK.

The game had worried me for all sorts of reasons: Auburn's defense was iffy, and despite the growing number of injuries suffered by Georgia, it still had quarterback Aaron Murray and running back Todd Gurley. But overcoming a 20-point lead wasn't going to be easy for Georgia, especially on the road. In my mind, I had already moved on to the night game between State and Bama.

When we landed in Charlotte, I turned on my phone, checked the score and nearly jumped out of the plane as it taxied. Sure enough, Murray had thrown a pair of touchdown passes to cut the lead to 37–31, with six minutes left to play. I had to see the finish.

When the plane door opened, I made like Herschel Walker and sprinted past everyone in line. *Sorry about that, folks.* I found a sports bar, and there it was, my worst viewing nightmare:

The NASCAR Nationwide Series Ford EcoBoost 300 from the Homestead-Miami Speedway.

Only in Charlotte.

I found another sports bar and it was the same thing: NASCAR.

I broke a land-speed record running to the USAir lounge and got here just in time to watch as Murray, on fourth and goal, scrambled five yards up the middle and powered his way into the end zone to tie the game. The extra point gave Georgia a 1-point lead with 1:49 remaining to play.

A Florida fan starts talking to me as Auburn gets the ball back for the final drive. Yes, just what I need: a Gator in my ear. The Tigers begin at their own 22-yard line, move to their 35 and then stall. There is a loss of two yards on first down, an incomplete pass on second down and a sack for a six-yard loss on third down. Now it is fourth and 18 on the Tigers' 27. Auburn is doomed.

Gus Malzahn takes a time-out.

Then Mark Richt takes a time-out.

If this doesn't end soon, I'm going to be *driving* to Birmingham.

As Tigers quarterback Nick Marshall takes the shotgun snap, I see just three Georgia rushers and then picket lines of Bulldog defenders in the secondary. UGA has Auburn's receivers outnumbered.

I hear CBS's Verne Lundquist say, "Lets it go," as Marshall steps up and releases the pass from his own 20.

I say to the Gator fan, "No way."

The pass travels nearly sixty yards in the air and then—and I still can't believe it—two Georgia defenders collide and tip the ball forward. That's when Auburn's Ricardo Louis, who seems to have lost track of the caromed ball, somehow taps it in the air several times before finally pulling it close as he crosses the goal line with just twenty-five seconds left to play.

I stand there in disbelief. So does Georgia's Murray, who slams his white ballcap against the turf. Has there ever been a quarterback who has lost in more painful ways than Murray? Remember the defeat against Alabama in the 2012 SEC Championship, when time ran out before the Bulldogs could run one last play? And now this.

Lundquist, who has made a career of being at the right places at the right times (at Augusta National in 1986 for the "Yessir!" call as forty-six-year-old Jack Nicklaus birdied No. 17 during his winning

Sunday charge; at the Meadowlands in 1992, when Duke's Christian Laettner sank a last-second, game-winning shot against Kentucky in the NCAA East Regional Final; at the Masters again in 2005 for Tiger Woods's chip-in at No. 16), lets the moment breathe and simply says, "Talk about a Hail Mary."

Broadcast partner Gary Danielson calls it "the play of the year . . . the most improbable touchdown you'll ever see . . . a miracle of miracles."

Georgia still has twenty-five seconds left, but it doesn't matter. There will be no miracle of miracles for the Bulldogs. My Iron Bowl matchup still lives.

There is a miracle of miracles for me. I make my flight.

I'm going to talk down Bama, I'm going to talk up Auburn.
If Paul Finebaum gets in the way and says something, I'm
going to threaten him with a country-boy ass whuppin'.

—CHARLES FROM REELTOWN

CHAPTER 16

War Eagle, Roll Tide

Saturday, November 23, 2013
Stillwater, Oklahoma

THE SEASON SKINNY: Saban's reaction to AJ McCarron gracing the cover of *Sports Illustrated*: "Do you think I sit around all day looking at magazines, or what?" . . . Oregon and Baylor's BCS chances are officially dead–Ducks lose at Arizona, Bears lose at Oklahoma State. Baylor, which hasn't beaten an AP-ranked team on the road since 1991, began the week at No. 4 in BCS Standings, Oregon at No. 5. . . . *GameDay* sign in Stillwater: "Finebaum Lives With His Mom." . . . Despite a loss to Arizona State, UCLA freshman linebacker and running back Myles Jack is officially a star. . . . A 3.7-magnitude earthquake hits Stillwater on Friday, which is less than the 5.6 quake that hit the city in November 2011–Herbstreit was here for both. . . . It's the twenty-nine-year anniversary of Doug Flutie's Hail Mary pass against Miami. . . . Florida hits a new low, losing to Georgia Southern.

In late 2010, I was asked to give a eulogy for a friend of mine—a devout and longtime Alabama fan who had died shortly before Auburn was to play Oregon in the BCS National Championship Game. So devoted was he to Alabama football that he used to visit Bear Bryant's grave site every September 11—the Bear's birthday. More than anything, my friend despised Auburn.

I was the second of two eulogists at the funeral service. Preceding me was a man who began to tell a story about the final moments of my friend's life. Everybody at the service, including myself, leaned forward in his or her seat.

The eulogist explained that my friend had spent his last days in hospice care. A nurse had stood mournful watch. As the time approached, my friend's sister had stepped to bed's edge to say her final goodbyes. Tears welled in her eyes as she told her brother, "I love you."

My friend, recounted the eulogist, had half-whispered something into his sister's ear. His dying words, the last he would ever speak, were . . .

"Go Ducks."

If only every Alabama-Auburn story were that innocently absurd.

For instance, when I met Harvey Almorn Updyke Jr. this past June in Opelika, Alabama, it was hard to think of him as the most famous man in the Lee County Detention Center and the most infamous fan in college football.

When he walked through the door for our scheduled visit, he was fifty pounds lighter than the last time I had seen him. His thinning, dull blond hair was longer, though, and he had grown a thick, bushy handlebar mustache that gave him a *Sons of Anarchy* look.

His flip-flops made a small squeaking noise on the floor, and on the chest-high pocket of his county-issued orange jumpsuit he wore an unauthorized message over his heart. *"Roll Damn Tide,"* it said, scrawled unevenly in black ink.

We hugged. Actually, I did most of the hugging; Harvey was wearing handcuffs. This was his seventy-sixth and final day in jail. He would be released the following day from a facility whose official Web site features a photo of the Lee County sheriff posing in front of the 2010 BCS National Championship trophy, won by Auburn, and another photo of the school's mascot, Aubie the Tiger, standing on a Lee County Sheriff's patrol car.

"My wife wants me to read a statement tomorrow when I get out, apologizing for what I have done and saying my fifteen minutes of shame are up," said Harvey.

What he did was so shocking that not even the most fanatical Alabama followers have condoned it. Well, maybe *the most* fanatical have.

And somehow I was in the middle of it.

Some background:

That BCS crystal trophy in the sheriff's photo was made possible by one of the greatest comebacks in Iron Bowl history. That was the year the No. 2–ranked Tigers trailed the 11th–ranked Tide, 24–0, late in the second quarter at Bryant-Denny Stadium.

Not much was at stake for Auburn—only a place in the national championship game, as well as the Heisman hopes of its quarterback Cam Newton, who had escaped the clutches of the NCAA after allegations that his father had essentially tried to sell his playing services to the highest bidder. (Allegations or not, some clever Bama stadium employee played the song "Take the Money and Run" over the Bryant-Denny loudspeakers during Auburn's pregame warm-up that year.)

What happened next is Iron Bowl legend. Newton threw three touchdown passes and ran for another as Auburn rallied to win, 28–27. Newton went on to win the Heisman and the Tigers went on to defeat favored Oregon in the national title game.

A year earlier it had been Alabama that had won it all. Now Bama fans had to endure not only the searing pain of a Tide home-field collapse in the Iron Bowl, but the images of the Tiger faithful draping the historic trees at Toomer's Corner—two 130-year-old, thirty-foot-high oaks—in toilet paper. And, of course, they would have to listen for month after month to the hyena-like taunts of Tiger fans.

Some Bama fans took the dignified approach and offered Auburn their reluctant congratulations. Some Bama fans seethed quietly and began the countdown to the 2011 Iron Bowl. One Bama fan took revenge.

On January 27, 2011, the call screener for our show typed, "Al from

Dadeville . . . Bear Bryant's death," on the studio monitor. I decided to take the call.

"Al is from Dadeville, Alabama. Hey, Al."

"Hey, Paul, how you doin'?"

Al began to recite an Alabama football old wives' tale: that Auburn students had viciously TP'd those same Toomer's Corner trees to celebrate Bear Bryant's death in 1982.

"Now stop, stop, stop, stop, stop," I said. "I just have the most difficult time ever believing that Auburn students rolled Toomer's Corner when the news broke that Coach Bryant died. Does anyone else remember that? I don't."

But "Al" insisted it was fact. He offered to send me a copy of a newspaper story detailing the supposed offense. I didn't come right out and call him a liar, but I said there was "no way that could be true."

Al was undeterred. He wanted to tell me a story, to build a case for some action that had not yet been made clear.

"This year," he said, "I was at the Iron Bowl and I saw where they put a Scam Newton jersey on Bear Bryant's statue."

I reminded Al that Bryant's been dead for twenty-eight years. My finger hovered on the kill button—a red X that I could push to take us to the next caller. I was this close to cutting off Al.

"Well, let me tell you what I did," said Al. "The weekend after the Iron Bowl, I went to Auburn, Alabama, because I live thirty miles away, and I poisoned the two Toomer's trees."

I laughed. "OK, well, that's fair."

"I put Spike 80DF in them," he said.

I didn't know Spike 80DF from Spike Lee but I assumed it was some sort of poison.

"Did they die?" I asked.

"Do what?"

"Did . . . they . . . die?"

"They're not dead yet," said Al, "but they definitely will die."

"Is that against the law to poison a tree?"

"Well, do you think I care?"

"Uh, no."

"I really don't. Roll Damn Tide."

Click.

It had been an entertaining and bizarre one minute and fifty-nine seconds of radio, but I figured it was another Bama crazy whose whole mission that day was to get a rise out of Auburn followers. You have to understand that the Toomer's Corner trees were sacred at Auburn. In Mafia terms, they were made men. To damage, desecrate or poison those trees was to wage holy war on all those who held Auburn dear to their hearts. It would be like serving Bevo for supper at a University of Texas alumni fund-raiser, or painting a giant eye patch on Notre Dame's Touchdown Jesus.

I might have thought Al's claims of poisoning the trees were fantasy, but the Department of Homeland Security thought otherwise. Soil samples were taken the next day, and Auburn later announced that a "very lethal dose" of a tree-killing herbicide had been discovered and that there was little long-term hope for the two oaks.

"Al" was really a sixty-two-year-old former Texas state trooper named Harvey Updyke. He was arrested and charged with assorted felonies and misdemeanors, and later pleaded not guilty by reason of mental disease or defect.

Harvey wasn't unlike a lot of Bama fans I have met or spoken with on the show. He was the first to have ever poisoned an opposing school's trees, but his utter devotion to Bama wasn't unusual.

The national media portrayed him as a lunatic. After all, what kind of person kills trees out of spite? What kind of person has an entire Bama wardrobe? What kind of person names one of his children Bear Bryant and another Crimson Tyde (and would have named another child Ally Bama if only his wife had capitulated)?

But Harvey was more like the rest of Bama's die-hard fans than the outside world could ever know. In 2012, seventy-six baby girls in the United States were named Crimson, Krimson or Krymson. Thirty-five of those girls were from Alabama. In that same year, nine baby boys in the state were named Crimson. Six were named Auburn.

See what I'm getting at? In the context of the Bama-Auburn rivalry, at least, Harvey was no freak. His actions were deplorable, reprehensible and grotesque, but they shouldn't have come as a complete surprise. There are some extremist Bama fans who supported the spirit of his actions, if not the poisoning itself.

His was arguably the most famous caller to a sports talk radio show in history. The story became a national sensation and since Harvey wasn't talking anymore, all the major TV networks began asking *me* to appear on their programs.

Most of the people asking the questions knew very little about college football and even less about the anatomy of the Bama-Auburn rivalry. To understand it, you had to live it.

Harvey called the show again in April 2011. His first call had lasted less than two minutes. This one lasted forty-five.

"I'd like to apologize to my children, the University of Alabama and my high school coach," Harvey said.

He didn't apologize to Auburn. Instead he said he regretted phoning my show back in January to brag about the poisoning, calling it "one of the biggest mistakes I ever made in my life. All my adult life my wives kind of said I'm a crap-stirrer. I like to stir crap. I was just trying to upset the Auburn Nation. Paul, I never thought it'd come to this."

He kept talking.

"I don't want those trees to die. I would give anything in the world if that had never happened. I don't want my legacy to be the Auburn tree poisoner. I guess it's too late now."

Before he hung up, I asked him what he would say to Auburn fans who wanted their pound of his flesh.

"If I was an Auburn fan, I would be upset too," he said. "I just want to tell them I'm not a bad person. I'm an Alabama fan. Tommy Lewis and the '54 Cotton Bowl. He came off the bench and tackled the Rice player. They asked him, 'Why'd you do it?' He said, 'I just have too much Bama in me.' Too full of Bama.

"To the Auburn people, I don't blame them. I'm gonna get what I deserve."

But then the supposedly apologetic Harvey reversed course.

"This is gonna make people mad, but I gotta do it," he said. "Roll Damn Tide."

That was in April. Twenty-three months later he pleaded guilty to felony criminal damage of an agricultural facility. Harvey was doing his time and now there we were, hugging in June 2013.

Our meeting was weeks in the making. Sheriff Jay Jones approved the meeting under the condition that it wasn't media-related. Since I was a man without a radio program or employer (it wouldn't be until that May that I joined ESPN), I qualified. Another stipulation was that the contents of the interview not be revealed for a minimum of a year, or until this book was published.

On the way to the jail, I stopped at a local Books-A-Million store and bought Harvey two preseason football magazines so that he could thumb through them while he was locked up (if not while we spoke). Each inmate had three pairs of plain white underwear, three pairs of plain white socks, three plain white T-shirts and one pair of plain white tennis shoes. Upon request, an inmate would be issued a Bible or Koran. And apparently a pair of flip-flops.

Harvey missed his freedom and his family, but what he said he missed most was walking his dog: Nick Saban.

I was told Harvey was housed in the "safe" part of the jail, but he said he had had several brushes with other inmates and had a vast experience in getting his "ass whupped."

"When you get into a fight," he said, "you don't even feel the pain."

He might have been targeted by a few prisoners, presumably Auburn fans or arborists, but Harvey said he was a celebrity to most of the other inmates.

"I can't tell you how many times I signed autographs," he said.

He was paid for the autographs with the currency of that particular jail: Little Debbie Honey Buns.

We talked about the Tide's upcoming season. Harvey wanted to go over the entire Tide lineup. He wondered about the wide receivers. He raved about running back T. J. Yeldon. We talked about the issues he would be facing upon his release.

He said he had found religion in that jail-issued Bible. He said he had mellowed. I wanted to believe him, but I'm not sure I did. Something about the "Roll Damn Tide" tattoo on his biceps said otherwise. He was still reveling in his fifteen minutes. It was weird, pathetic, but mostly it was sad. He gave me his phone number. I wished him the best.

When he was released the next day from the detention center, Harvey did the impossible: he kept his mouth shut. I later jotted down the memorable parts of our conversation. The truth is, I have a soft spot for Harvey—not for what he did to those oak trees, but for his Bama passion, however incredibly misguided it was.

I never thought Harvey should be sent to jail. Fine him. Make him do community service. But having Harvey Updyke sit in jail trading autographs for Honey Buns served no purpose. Jail would never make Harvey less of an Alabama fan.

Harvey had too much Bama in him. But Bama has always had a weird effect on people.

Auburn fans are different. Auburn fans usually have a direct connection to the school, whereas Alabama fans, like Yankee fans or Notre Dame fans, don't necessarily have blood ties or lambskin degrees. But Auburn fans: they attended school there, or their relatives did, or they have a fondness for the underdog. Those who follow Auburn prefer to be called part of the Auburn "family." The die-hards will correct you every time you call them mere "fans," just like they corrected me the first time I mispronounced the name of their stadium. I called it "Jordan-Hare," as in, Michael Jordan. I learned quickly: it's "Jur-dan-Hare."

And the clichéd way to refer to members of that Auburn family is to say they have a chip on their shoulder, that they want Auburn to be Bama when the program grows up. That's wrong. Auburn folks are actually proud of that chip, proud that they're *not* Bama. They embrace their uniqueness. I think they even embrace their inferiority.

To me, Alabama is the Yankees. It is a program soaked in success, its hands weighed down by championship rings.

Auburn, to extend the baseball analogy, is the Chicago Cubs. OK, Auburn is more successful than the Cubbies (105 years, and counting, without a World Series championship), but it's Cub-like in its desperation to be a version of the Yankees. Cub-like in its occasional ineptitude.

I think it says a lot about Auburn that when it wanted to fire Tommy Tuberville, it put the president of the university, the athletic director and a bunch of trustees on a plane and didn't think the story was going to get out. Really?

I think it says something about Tuberville's good fortune that he just happened to be friends with the pilot of the private plane that was transporting the Auburn firing squad—and that the pilot told Tuberville, and Tuberville told everyone else and saved his job.

Auburn has had its successes, but it also has a history of tying its shoelaces together and then wondering why it always trips and falls.

In some ways, Auburn's ineptitude makes it lovable, just like the Cubs. The Tigers won the national championship in 2010, but what is that Auburn season best remembered for? The Iron Bowl comeback and the Newton eligibility controversy.

Do I think Newton's dad tried to shop his son's football services to the highest bidder? Yes, absolutely. Did Cam know about it? Well, it's hard to believe that he didn't have some inkling of what was going on. But I've never heard anybody make a compelling case that he did. The NCAA didn't have enough evidence to prove it, which is why Newton was allowed to continue playing.

I defended Cam Newton and Auburn. I had heard lots of accusations, lots of supposedly airtight theories, but I hadn't seen any actual ironclad evidence of wrongdoing.

Cam Newton was no different from a thousand other athletes who have been in the same position. You survive any way you can. But I wouldn't nominate him for a Nobel Prize. Did he skate the rules? Probably.

The NCAA never proved Auburn was involved. There were a lot of questions involving the case, but not a lot of answers. In the end, I think the NCAA, given what it could prove, had to let Newton play.

He is beloved at Auburn. He's not Bo Jackson–level beloved, but he's up there. They respect Cam because he won a Heisman and led Auburn to a national championship. But they love him because he beat Bama and caused the Tide long-lasting pain.

I have a neighbor who is an Auburn fan. After the Tigers won it all, he said, "I hope we didn't cheat. That would be disappointing as an Auburn graduate. But I certainly enjoyed the night, and I wouldn't trade it for anything."

Auburn fans don't care. They won the championship. They don't apologize for it. They're not giving the trophy back.

Still, even when Auburn wins a national title, the good feelings don't last long. Two years after the championship, the Tigers had the worst season in their history and fired the coach who had brought them the crystal trophy in the first place.

Chizik is an asterisk at Auburn. He is devoid of a legacy. It's like Newton drove the car and Chizik was a glove box accessory. He'll be associated with the national championship, but his name is written in disappearing ink. The championship was all about Cam, but the downfall was all about Chizik.

There are pockets of Auburn fans outside of Auburn, but you can't drive anywhere in the state of Alabama without seeing a Bama cap or bumper sticker. From a pure percentage ratio, I bet you there are more Bama fans in that state than there are Ohio State fans in Ohio, or Michigan fans in Michigan.

The late Beano Cook put it best. He said Bama-Auburn was the football equivalent of Gettysburg South. They live next to each other and they despise each other.

There has always been a rivalry between Auburn and Alabama, but it didn't get hot as a pancake skillet until Pat Dye and Bo Jackson started beating Bama. For the first time in modern football history, Bama was at a disadvantage.

Bear Bryant was dead. His successor, Ray Perkins, stayed just four seasons before taking the Tampa Bay Buccaneers head coaching job.

Had Bama asked me for my advice back then (as fat a chance then as it is now or ever), I would have told them to hire Miami's Howard Schnellenberger instead of Perkins. Schnellenberger had a history with the Bear. It was Bryant who had recruited him to Kentucky (Schnellenberger would become an all-American after Bryant left UK for Bama). It was Bryant who had hired him as an assistant coach at Bama. And it was Bryant who had instructed Schnellenberger to bring back a quarterback from Pennsylvania named Joe Namath.

Perkins rubbed people the wrong way, but if you're going to be honest about his brief tenure, he did leave the program in better shape than he found it. I'm convinced that had Schnellenberger gotten the job, there would have never been the need to hire another head coach in 1987.

This is where Bama screwed up again. Instead of hiring Alabama native (and, briefly, Bama quarterback) Bobby Bowden, whom Bryant had always liked and whom he'd helped when Bowden was the coach at nearby Samford University, the school hired Bill Curry, Georgia-born, Georgia Tech–educated and without a single connection to Bama or the Bear. I was covering the story for the *Post-Herald*. Bowden wanted the job, interviewed for the job (Bowden in the morning, Curry in the afternoon) and everyone thought he was going to get the job. At one point, there was a local report that Bowden was on the brink of closing the deal.

But as the day dragged on, Bowden returned home to Tallahassee, with still no news. Something just didn't seem right, so I called him that night at home.

"I haven't heard anything" said Bowden.

Later in the evening, I reached a member of the Alabama board of trustees.

"All I can tell you is that it's not going to be Bowden," he said.

"You've got to be kidding," I said. I was stunned.

"We just felt after interviewing Coach Bowden that he had too much baggage."

"Too much 'baggage'?" I said. "What does that mean?"

The trustee paused for a moment. "He's simply too old."

Too old?

It was a ridiculous miscalculation. Bowden had turned fifty-seven two months earlier. He was twelve years younger than Bryant when the Bear died. Beginning in 1987 and through 2000, Bowden's FSU teams would win at least ten games and finish in the top five of the rankings each season. He would win national championships in 1993 and 1999 and would become the all-time leader in major-college career victories.

Instead, they got Curry, who was the anti-Perkins: a nice guy, good talker, great schmoozer. But he wasn't the coach Bowden was—and never would be.

Next came Stallings, who looked a bit like Bryant, sounded a bit like Bryant and in 1992, when Bama won the national title, even coached a bit like Bryant. But during his first season at Bama, the Tide finished 7-5.

So in all, we're talking about eight wasted seasons for Alabama. Eight seasons during which Auburn found its footing and gained confidence.

From 1982 through 1989, Auburn beat Alabama six out of eight times. Not since the birth of the rivalry some hundred years earlier had Auburn had that kind of football success against Bama.

Stallings put an end to the Auburn domination, beating the Tigers three consecutive times and five of seven during his tenure.

Stallings was a good hire, but facts are facts: NCAA violations were committed during his tenure—specifically, rule-breaking arrangements, including loans between players and agents. The NCAA's Committee on Infractions described Alabama's response to the situation as "a distressing failure of institutional control." The sanctions included scholarship reductions, probation, a loss of scholarships and a postseason ban.

One time I questioned the truth-telling ability of Stallings relative to the case, and in short order received a scathing letter from his wife. She wanted me to know that Gene was the most honest man in the world and would never lie about anything, let alone his conduct in this matter. Years later I emceed a banquet in his honor and joked about that letter to the crowd of 800. Afterward, Stallings's wife gave me a hug. I thought my eyes were going to pop out.

Stallings did win that national championship, but those NCAA violations contributed to his decision to resign after the 1996 season. Bama then entered the dark ages.

His successor, Bama defensive coordinator Mike DuBose, was completely out of his depth. When allegations surfaced in 1999 that he was having an affair with his secretary—allegations that DuBose publicly declared as "unfounded rumors and innuendos"—his wife, Polly, agreed to let me interview her. She did one of those good-wife, stand-by-your-man routines where she insisted her husband could have never done what he was accused of doing. About two months later, DuBose admitted publicly that he had. Incredibly, the school, which paid the secretary a settlement fee of $350,000, allowed DuBose to remain as coach. He was fired after a 3-8 season in 2000 (Bama's worst record in more than four decades) and an overall record of 24-23. Fourteen months later, the NCAA would send a preliminary letter of inquiry to the school as part of its initial investigation into alleged major rule infractions by Tide boosters during DuBose's tenure.

Dennis Franchione (17-8 before he bolted to Texas A&M without bothering to meet with his Tide players in person)? Mike Price (hired in late December 2002, gone by May 2003 after a strip club controversy cost him his job and a seven-year, $10 million contract)? Mike Shula (26-23; four consecutive losses to Auburn)?

So many Crimson Tide embarrassments. So much national ridicule. Alabama needed a tourniquet to stop the hemorrhaging.

Saban was hired in 2007 to repair and restore the reputation of the program, but even he lost his first Iron Bowl, meaning Auburn had won six in a row against the Tide.

So that's the Alabama coaching history lesson as it relates to Auburn's rise. It was during the post-Bear era that Pat Dye began to assert himself in the rivalry and that Bama was given no choice but to finally play a game at Jordan-Hare Stadium (Dye led the Tigers to the historic 1989 win).

Dye was smart and savvy. He was the one who laid the framework and provided the blueprint for how to compete with and beat Bama. Blueprints are nice; Bo Jackson was better.

Of all the things Dye did during his twelve seasons at Auburn, somehow prying Vincent Edward Jackson out of Bessemer, Alabama (just forty-five miles away from the Bama campus), has to rank in the top three. Top one?

I played a small part in the drama.

In the spring of Bo's senior year at McAdory High School, I did a story dealing with the delicate topic of how much longer Bryant would coach at Alabama. Bryant had won a national title in 1979, but then dropped to ten wins in 1980 and nine in 1981. He entered 1982 needing a bounce-back year, and to have that he needed to sign Jackson, who had grown up a Bama fan.

My story came out during the heart of recruiting season and was accompanied by a close-up photo of Bryant's weathered, creviced face. He was sixty-eight years old at the time, and he looked every day of it, and maybe more.

Several Alabama assistant coaches had told me privately that they were looking to leave the program. Things were beginning to unravel, to the point that when I spoke with Bo's mother, she said she wasn't going to let her son go to Tuscaloosa.

Dye, who had starred at Georgia but coached for Bryant at Bama, will deny it now, but he told me later that he made sure every high school coach and Auburn-targeted recruit in the state received a copy of my story—with that unflattering photo of Bryant.

Bo chose Auburn. Another high-profile Bama recruit also chose the Tigers at the last moment, meaning the unthinkable had happened: Bryant had missed out on arguably the two best players in the Birmingham area.

Nobody knew Bo would eventually win the Heisman Trophy, then become a cultural icon and one of the greatest athletes in the history of American sports. What we did know, however, was that a really good running back who had adored Alabama as a kid had decided to go to an Auburn program just coming off probation and in the middle of a shaky transition. (Years later, Jackson would write in his autobiography that Alabama had bungled his recruiting, beginning with Bryant's suggesting that he might be switched to defense. He also wrote that then–Tide assistant coach Ken Donahue had told

Jackson he wouldn't see significant playing time as a running back until his junior year at Alabama.)

The inability to sign Jackson was a big deal, and I could see the writing on the Alabama wall. Tide fans didn't want to admit it, but the Bryant dynasty was coming to an end. They'd thought those national titles in 1978 and 1979 and a serious run at another championship in 1980 guaranteed the program perpetual success.

In the middle to late 1970s, Auburn was the program that couldn't shoot straight. But in Dye's second year, 1982, he beat the Bear in Birmingham. He beat Bama again in 1983 and should have beaten the Tide another time in 1984, except that Jackson ran the wrong way on a goal-line play that cost the Tigers the game and a Sugar Bowl appearance.

Auburn had a late lead in 1985, but Bama's Van Tiffin kicked a record 52-yard field goal as time—and the Tigers—expired. And then Dye won the next four Iron Bowls.

The truth is, Auburn could have/should have won eight Iron Bowls in a row. And when it beat Bama that very first time at Jordan-Hare in 1989, it was a religious experience. The Auburn fans were screaming at the top of their lungs an hour before kickoff—and kept screaming throughout the entire game. I'd never seen anything like it.

When Dye, who had helped pressure Bama to end the Jordan-Hare boycott, won that game, his Auburn legacy was forever secure. In fact, it might have been secure the minute Bama's players set foot on the Auburn home field.

Dye compared the sight of an Alabama team at Jordan-Hare to the fall of the Berlin Wall. I was surprised Dye even knew the Berlin Wall had fallen less than a month earlier.

One of my favorite Dye stories happened on our show about six years ago. By then, Dye was a regular on the show, and one day I said to him on the air, "Coach, I understand you had an interesting visit the other day."

"I sure did, Paul," said Dye. "I went to Monroeville, Alabama, and got to meet Harper Lee."

Lee is the Pulitzer Prize–winning author of *To Kill a Mockingbird* who was born and raised in Monroeville and had attended Alabama. She wasn't a college football fan, but as Dye told a relative who helped arrange the meeting, he wasn't an avid reader of "no damned literature."

The reclusive Lee spent three hours with the Auburn coach and agreed to autograph a copy of her famed book, which Dye, with Lee's permission, later auctioned off to benefit the Auburn School of Nursing.

He admitted he had never read the book in school, but had read it after retiring from coaching.

And then he said something I'll never forget:

"I'm going to treasure that book, *To Kill a Blackbird*, for the rest of my life."

The rivalry meant everything to Dye. It has always meant more to Auburn than it has to Alabama. That could change, but not until Auburn starts beating the Tide on a regular basis again.

Auburn, in Terry Bowden's first season, finished undefeated in 1993, but Bama backed into the SEC Championship Game because the Tigers were on NCAA probation. Auburn ended DuBose's Bama coaching career with a loss in 2000. It beat Bama on its way to an unbeaten season in 2004. It sacked Bama quarterback Brodie Croyle eleven times in a 2005 victory. It shocked Bama in the 2010 Camback.

Some of those Alabama coaches had no business ever being hired. Shula in 2003? He got the job because of his last name and because of his ties to the school (he was a decent quarterback for the Tide). The guy who should have gotten the job instead of Shula was Sylvester Croom, who was born and raised in Tuscaloosa and was twice the Alabama player (he was an all-American for Bryant) that Shula was, and who was later an assistant coach for Bryant. We had Reverend Jesse Jackson on the show to talk about why Alabama should hire Croom, who would have become the first African-American head football coach in the SEC—a decision I think the Bear himself would have applauded.

But even aside from that, Croom—a Tuscaloosa native, an Alabama all-American, a former NFL player, an Alabama assistant coach, a longtime NFL assistant—was richly qualified for the job.

A lot of people in Alabama didn't want to hear from Jackson, and neither did they want Croom to get the job. Some even dropped the N-word. We had a delay mechanism on the show, but I made the decision to let the word go. Our listeners could learn from a caller's ignorance.

Croom was a finalist for the job, but in the end Alabama chose Shula. It was a missed opportunity. I've always argued that, in addition to the on-field benefits, Croom would have been a welcome sign of progress in the state of Alabama, particularly on the fortieth anniversary of Governor George Wallace's civil rights trampling inauguration: "Segregation now, segregation tomorrow, segregation forever."

I think Bama liked Croom, but didn't want to deal with the controversy and publicity that would accompany the hiring of the first African-American football coach in the seventy-one-year history of the SEC. Bama was wary and weary of it all.

So Bama played it safe. It chose the second-born of the famous Don Shula. If only it had turned out to be a like-father-like-son kind of deal.

Croom was hired in late 2003 as head coach at Mississippi State, where the chances of success were significantly lower than they were at football-rich Bama (and where they were even lower after the NCAA hit the Bulldogs' program with sanctions related to Jackie Sherrill's tenure there). Then again, Shula—who admittedly had to navigate the effects of Bama's booster-related NCAA probation and two-year postseason ban—finished 4-9 in his first season on the sidelines.

In 2005, when Shula led Bama to a 10-2 record (but lost the Iron Bowl) and Mississippi State University suffered through its second straight 3-8 season under Croom, I heard from lots of Tide followers who said I owed Shula an apology. Bama, they said, had made the right hire.

They weren't saying it in 2006, when Bama lost six of its last nine regular-season games. One of those losses came at home against Croom's undermanned Mississippi State team.

I don't take sides very often at football games, but, to put it mildly, I was pulling hard for Croom that day at Bryant-Denny Stadium. There's no cheering in the press box, but I was cheering to myself when Mississippi State won, 24–16.

I wasn't rooting against Shula and Bama, but for Croom. (By the way, Croom beat Saban a year later too.)

The loss to Croom all but ended Shula's Bama career. He lost to LSU a week later and to Auburn the next week. He was fired the day after the Iron Bowl defeat.

During Gene Chizik's first season at Auburn, 2009, we had an attorney on the show who intimated that the Tigers' program was out of control and that there was a growing thug factor on the team. It obviously wasn't a positive portrayal of the program, and Auburn fans reacted accordingly, which is to say that they took it out on me.

The Iron Bowl was at Jordan-Hare that year. Before the game, I met up with Taylor Hicks, of *American Idol* fame, and we headed to a tailgate party with a police escort. Of course, that didn't stop Auburn fans from yelling and spitting at me. I did my best to ignore it.

The policeman assigned to Taylor leaned toward him and said, "Who the hell is this guy you're with? *He's* the one who needs protection."

Later, when it was time to enter the stadium through the press gate, an Auburn fan stormed toward me, got right in my face and started to swear at me. I wouldn't acknowledge him, which made him even madder. Moments before it looked like he was going to throw a punch at me, a couple of guys wedged themselves between us.

"If you take another step toward Paul," said one of them to the fan, "you're going down."

Chizik's first Iron Bowl as a head coach didn't end as happily. Auburn led No. 2–ranked Bama midway through the fourth quarter, but couldn't stop quarterback Greg McElroy as he led a late Tide comeback with a fifteen-play scoring drive. Auburn had lost not only the Iron Bowl, but the chance to ruin Bama's undefeated season (the Tide would go on to win the national championship).

Afterward, as I was killing time before doing a TV appearance at the stadium, Jonna Chizik spotted me as I stood in a room reserved for Auburn recruits.

I had met her a few times in the past and she had always been pleasant enough. This time she just stared at me and finally said, "You have no idea the damage you do to college football."

"I'm sorry, what?"

For the next several minutes she tore into me. Considering the day I'd had, her lecture on what a louse I was didn't seem so bad.

I listened politely and then said, "Mrs. Chizik, with all due respect, I really don't know your husband that well."

"And you're never going to get to know him, either," she said.

By this point, we were nose to nose. I was trying to be respectful of who she was, but it was time to end the confrontation.

"Listen," I said, "I have some close friends who are coaches." I was going to tell her that through those friendships I'd come to understand the pressures that coaches and their families felt every day. But before I could say another word, she said sarcastically, "Oh, yes, we know what good friends you are with Nick and Terry Saban."

And the ten-minute verbal beat-down resumed.

So you see, Harvey Updyke isn't the only nut job in that Bama-Auburn universe.

We're this way all year long. If I run into a BAM, I say, "War Eagle." If they see my Auburn shirt, they say those ugly words. And BAM stands for, "Bama Ass Moron." You put an S on the back of Moron and that takes care of 'em all.

—TAMMY

CHAPTER 17

In Gus We Trust

Saturday, November 30, 2013

Auburn, Alabama

THE SEASON SKINNY: BCS Standings entering the Iron Bowl: Alabama, Florida State, Ohio State, Auburn, Missouri. . . . Thanksgiving week results: Texas beats Texas Tech, still can win Big 12. . . . Arkansas drops to 0-8 in the SEC. . . . Tennessee beats Kentucky to avoid its first-ever eight-loss season. . . . Florida loses to FSU, ends season at 4-8 . . . Missouri wins SEC East. . . . The Head Ball Coach beats Clemson a fifth straight time. . . . 2012 regular season BCS No. 1 Notre Dame finishes 2013 regular season with loss to Stanford and 8-4 record. . . . Fourth consecutive week a top-five BCS team loses a game.

It really comes down to this: if you were a Bama woman and the future of the human race depended on it, would you have sex with an Auburn man?

I can already hear Bama women everywhere saying, "Ewwww . . . gross." So I will take that as a no? (On the other hand, it's useless to reverse the question, because Auburn men would have sex with anyone.)

I have spent years trying to explain the Auburn-Alabama football rivalry to outsiders. I've appeared in documentaries. Been quoted in the nation's great newspapers. Tried to articulate it on my own radio show. But it's like trying to teach someone how to play the harp with his earlobes. It can't be done.

First of all, to call it a rivalry is to cheapen it. Tonya Harding and

Nancy Kerrigan were rivals. Tiger and Phil are rivals. Chiquita and Dole are rivals.

Alabama and Auburn are enemies. They're the Visigoths vs. the Romans. The Klingons vs. the Federation. You can cut the football hatred with the talons of War Eagle VII.

It is as unhealthy as secondhand smoke. It is generational, mean-spirited, and everlasting. But without it, I'm not sure I'd have a show.

To me, it is just so darned cute when other schools insist their rivalry game is better than Alabama-Auburn. I listen politely as they go on and on about Michigan–Ohio State, Army-Navy, USC–Notre Dame, Texas-Oklahoma, Cal-Stanford, Harvard-Yale, Wabash-DePauw, etc., but eventually you have to put these people in their place and out of their misery.

To be as clear as Cam Newton's plastic visor, there is no better or more bitter football rivalry/war than Alabama-Auburn. There is no rivalry that matches its intensity, its history and its effect on an entire state. There is no rivalry that creates more heroes, more goats or more ex-coaches. It has lost touch with reality and perspective. It weighs much too heavily on the minds of those who play in it and of those who live for it.

Let me try to explain the ferocity of the Iron Bowl to you:

When I worked in Birmingham, I used to date a woman who was an Auburn fan. I once asked her, "Why do you hate Alabama so much?"

She said, "When I was growing up in the seventies, I would get on the school bus and the kids who rooted for Alabama would make fun of me. They'd pepper me with spitballs. Harass me. And it was all because Alabama had won nine straight against Auburn. What kind of people do that?"

Alabama people do. But when Auburn won four in a row against Bama in the late '80s and then five in a row in the early to mid-2000s, Tigers fans were equally insufferable.

I went to the family home of my girlfriend that Thanksgiving.

They lived on a farm—she was my first, and last, farm girl. So that Thanksgiving night, after we were finished with dinner, my girl-friend's mother said, "Why don't we go into the parlor and listen to a record on the phonograph." This was 1987 and they were still listening to records on phonographs? I was almost forty years old, but thought I'd gone back to the days of the Glenn Miller Orchestra.

Except that they didn't want to listen to music. They wanted to listen to a recording of the 1972 Iron Bowl, forever known as "Punt Bama Punt." That's the game where Auburn trailed second-ranked Bama, 16–3, but then blocked two consecutive Tide punts, returned them both for touchdowns and won, 17–16.

I watched their faces as they listened to the game. It was as if they were hearing it for the very first time. They were so proud of that win.

Of course, I didn't want to mention to the family that Auburn had lost the next nine Iron Bowls after that 1972 game. Or that nobody churned their own ice cream anymore. Still, maybe they were on to something. The day after Thanksgiving, Auburn beat Bama, 10–0.

I don't want to bore you with a history lesson, but the Iron Bowl is where Bear Bryant won his 315th game and passed Amos Alonzo Stagg to become, at the time, the winningest major-college coach; where Bo Jackson went over the top, where he went bye-bye and where he went the wrong way; where Bama's Van Tiffin kicked a game-winning 52-yard field goal; where 96 years after the first Iron Bowl, Auburn fi-nally got to play the game at Jordan-Hare . . . and won, which caused its longtime sports information director to weep openly on the field; where Bama's Croyle was sacked eleven times; where Auburn and Cam Newton trailed, 24–0, and won, 28–27.

The Iron Bowl is a 365-day obsession of Bama and Auburn fans. It is the rivalry that once caused Bryant to refer to Auburn as "that cow college on the other side of the state." It is the reason why nobody in the state schedules a wedding or baptism (or, sure, a bar mitzvah) for late No-vember. It is the leading cause of arguments, to say nothing of divorces.

"In Alabama we only got two things that matter," I've heard Auburn alum Charles Barkley say. "That's Alabama and Auburn."

Those other rivalries have their moments—in a harmless, junior varsity kind of way. But the University of Michigan isn't in the same state as the Buckeyes. Auburn and Alabama share the same driver's licenses, the same borders, the same grocery store aisles.

Harvard-Yale takes place in a league that hasn't had a team ranked in a major-college poll since 1970, hasn't had a Heisman Trophy winner since 1951.

USC–Notre Dame can be fun, but it's not like Notre Dame's players grow up wanting nothing more than to beat the Trojans.

OU-Texas has the fancy nickname (the "Red River Rivalry"), but again, I refer you to the Two-State Theory. Plus, OU-Texas is played on a neutral field, with the tickets divided evenly. Yecch.

I'm a huge supporter of our armed forces and I love the pageantry and intensity of the Army-Navy game. But mostly I'm curious if someone from Army is going to kidnap the Navy goat. By the way, Army last won a national championship in 1946 and Navy never has.

Cal-Stanford . . . you know what? Never mind.

Nope, the rivalry that matters most is located where the stars fall.

Roll Tide. War Eagle.

As we begin the countdown to the 2013 Iron Bowl (my thirty-fourth, by the way), I keep saying that this is the biggest Bama-Auburn game of all time. I see their records (11-0 Bama, 10-1 Auburn), their rankings (No. 1 Tide, No. 4 Tigers) and their resolve. But no matter how many times I say it on the radio show or in interviews, I don't see Alabama losing to Auburn.

Yes, the game is at Jordan-Hare. Yes, this isn't the same Auburn team that started the season unranked and unnoticed. Yes, I keep telling anyone who will listen that it will be an "epic" game, perhaps the best ever. But even though this is only the second time both teams enter the game ranked in the AP top five, I'm not sure I believe my own hype of the matchup.

No matter what happens, Malzahn has my Coach of the Year vote. I had thought Auburn would be lucky to win eight games in 2013. And if the Tigers did win eight, I thought, they should throw a parade for the team. Instead, they've reached double-digit wins before meeting Bama.

The general Tide vibe is this: "Let's get this thing over with, move on to the SEC Championship and then win another national title. Auburn is good, but it's not Bama good." Plus, Bama fans remember the last two Alabama Iron Bowl victories, won by a combined 91–14 score. Auburn hasn't scored an offensive touchdown against the Tide since the fourth quarter of the 2010 Iron Bowl.

Every indicator points toward a Bama victory: In the previous three seasons, Auburn hadn't played in a game where both teams were ranked in the top ten. Bama had played in eight such games and won seven of them. The wise guys in Vegas have made Bama a 10½-point favorite.

My extremist Bama callers are saying Auburn is lucky to be in this position, that you only get one "Prayer at Jordan-Hare" per decade, if that. They are dismissing Auburn's chances partly because of the Prayer, partly because of Bama's 49–0 win against the Tigers a season earlier and partly because, no matter what, Bama fans will forever look at Auburn as their little brother. And little brothers aren't supposed to beat up big brothers.

I did my Friday show from a room inside a deserted Auburn Student Center. Everything was closed because of the Thanksgiving holidays. Still, you could feel the excitement building in town for the game. The game felt supersized, felt important.

It is an important moment for me too. I had been in Tuscaloosa a few weeks earlier with the *GameDay* crew for the LSU-Bama game. Now I'm at Auburn for the Iron Bowl, a rivalry and a game that had helped put my radio show on the map. This was the state and these were the two teams that had defined my show.

When I walk out to the *GameDay* set for my usual early Saturday morning *SportsCenter* hit, it is one of the great experiences of my life. I get booed. I always get booed. If I didn't get booed at Auburn, then it wouldn't be Auburn.

But I don't care. I love the passion of the crowd. I love the energy. This is one of the few times in my career that I take a moment and savor the scene. And my gosh, what a scene.

Auburn fans hope the Tigers can win, but most of them feel the same way I do: Bama is the better team. The phrase I hear most is "We're playing with house money." In other words, they can live with whatever happens against Bama—well, they can live with anything except another 49–0 beat-down.

When it comes time to pick a winner, I take Bama, 31–20, and don't think twice about it. The Auburn fans boo again, but I'm not sure their hearts are in it. I think they know Bama can actually win by a bigger margin.

After my segments on *GameDay* end, I walk over to the show's hospitality bus and talk with Charles Barkley, the guest picker for the show. Charles and I have a long history with lots of ups and a few downs. He's questioned my bona fides over the years, and is never happy when I take shots at Auburn. The last time I checked, he wasn't mad at me anymore. But that can change.

Nobody can hold court like Sir Charles. He takes a phone call from Malzahn. He talks about his high school football career (he lasted one day before quitting). He chats with his buddy Taylor Hicks. Then he goes out to the set and picks Auburn to upset Bama. And he doesn't do it as an Auburn homer, but as someone who sees something in the

Tigers (and maybe the Tide too) that makes him think an upset is possible.

Coach Corso doesn't agree. When it comes time for the headgear, out comes the mascot elephant head.

I go up to the stadium press box about an hour or so before the game. That's when I see Terry Saban ("Miss Terry," as Nick calls his wife of forty-plus years), who has recently been quoted in the *Wall Street Journal*, "You come to a crossroads and the expectations get so great, people get spoiled by success and there gets to be a lack of appreciation. We're kind of there now."

Saban *has* spoiled Bama fans. Then again, Bama fans are used to being spoiled. They think it is their birthright to win national championships.

What they don't understand is that those expectations are not only unrealistic, but destructive and suffocating. Nobody can function forever under those types of ridiculous expectations. Saban, who has lost only two games in the last three seasons, has dealt with those expectations since 2008. National championship or bust.

Terry's quotes were especially incendiary because of the timing of the story: the rumors of Saban replacing Mack Brown at Texas simply won't go away.

When Terry speaks, Alabama fans listen. Her comments made nervous Tide followers even more paranoid about the possibility of Saban bolting for the Longhorns. It also made some Alabama fans angry. In short, "How dare she question our expectations."

There was even a reader poll conducted by AL.com asking if Bama fans are spoiled by success. About 75 percent said yes. What a shock.

SEC commissioner Mike Slive is also in the press box. Along with *Sports Illustrated* college football writer Pete Thamel, we watch the end of the Ohio State–Michigan game together. If the unranked Wolverines can somehow upset the No. 3–ranked Buckeyes, it will all but guarantee that at least one SEC team will reach the national championship game. That explains why Slive watches the action and quietly says, "Go, go, go," when a Michigan runner breaks free.

As it stands, Alabama is No. 1 in the BCS Standings, followed by undefeated Florida State and then Ohio State. Auburn and Missouri are ranked Nos. 4 and 5. But if Auburn beats Bama, and FSU and Ohio State run the table, then the SEC will be a no-show in Pasadena for the BCS Championship.

Michigan, which trails by two touchdowns in the fourth quarter, rallies to move within 1 point with thirty-two seconds left to play. Rather than kick the game-tying extra point, the Wolverines are going for the 2-point conversion and the win. Slive looks more nervous than Michigan coach Brady Hoke.

Devin Gardner drops back for the final play, and Slive tries some body English as the Wolverines quarterback forces a pass into the end zone. The ball is intercepted and Ohio State leaves the Big House with a 42–41 win. A slightly despondent Slive walks away. The SEC's margin of error has just taken a hit.

Even with Ohio State's win, I consider an Alabama–Florida State national championship game a foregone conclusion. Earlier in the day, FSU beat an injury-decimated Florida team in its regular-season finale, and it will surely beat Duke in the ACC Championship. And Alabama will dispose of Auburn and then beat either Missouri or South Carolina in the SEC Championship. All will be right in the SEC world.

Even as Auburn takes a 7–0 first-quarter lead, I'm not worried. And I'm not worried when Alabama can't put the Tigers away after scoring 21 consecutive points in the second quarter. Instead, Bama gives up an Auburn touchdown shortly before halftime, and leads, 21–14.

OK, I am a little worried when Auburn ties the game, 21–21, in the third quarter. But then Bama answers: a 99-yard, Heisman-moment touchdown pass from AJ McCarron to Amari Cooper with 10:28 left in the game. I know how it will play out after that: Auburn will fold, and afterward Saban will say a victory is a victory, but complain about the Tide's inconsistencies (some knucklehead penalties, the missed field goals, the inability to put Auburn away in the first half). Bama fans will start booking their flights and hotel rooms in Pasadena—if they haven't already.

Any chance of an Auburn comeback ends a few minutes later, when Malzahn keeps his offense on the field for a fourth-and-one attempt at the Tigers' own 35. I keep thinking, "What is he doing?"

The Tide stuff Marshall for no gain. That means Bama gets the ball back deep in Auburn territory with 8:28 remaining. Game over.

Uh, not exactly.

Bama drives to the Auburn 13, but T. J. Yeldon gets nowhere on a third and one. Of course, Saban will send out the kicker Cade Foster and the field goal unit, get the 3 points from close distance (about thirty yards), take a 10-point lead with less than six minutes left and that will be that.

Instead, in a decision that I think will haunt Saban for the rest of his life, they hand the ball to Yeldon and again he fails to get the first down.

I'm not second-guessing Saban. I said it before it happened and I'm saying it after it happened: he should have tried the field goal. To me, it is arrogance that made him go for the first down. Saban was in position to almost certainly put the game out of reach with a field goal, but he overthought it. It will be the first of two disastrous decisions that cost him not only the Iron Bowl, but an opportunity for a third consecutive BCS title.

I know what Saban might say: that Foster's confidence was shot after missing a 44-yarder in the first quarter, and missing a 33-yarder and getting a 44-yarder blocked in the fourth quarter; that this is the same kicker who missed three of four field goal attempts in the 2011 overtime loss to LSU; that if he was going to roll the bones, he was going to do it with his rushing offense and not with a kicker who was in a fragile state.

I get it. I just don't agree with it.

Entering the game, Foster hadn't missed a field goal since September 21. And he did make a 28-yarder during Bama's first drive of the fourth quarter against Auburn. But a false start penalty against the Tide negated the field goal and he missed on the next play, the 33-yarder.

Once Auburn stops Yeldon on the fourth-down play, anything is possible. You almost get the sense that Alabama suddenly feels unsure of itself, that it is feeling the pressure after being unable to close out the game.

It's so loud in Jordan-Hare that the press box is shaking. And that's before Marshall hits Sammie Coates for a 39-yard TD pass that ties the score, 28–28, with thirty-two seconds remaining.

We are witnessing something incredible. Maybe Auburn *is* lucky. Or maybe they are simply mentally tougher than Alabama.

Auburn kicks off and Kenny Bell returns the ball 11 yards to the Bama 29. Twenty-five seconds are left—enough time for the senior quarterback McCarron to drive Bama into position for a game-winning field goal attempt. If that doesn't work, the game will go to overtime, where order will be restored and the Tide will quell the Auburn uprising. That's how we've been conditioned to think in recent years— Alabama will find a way to win. It always has. And as I think about it, I guess I'm guilty of having some of those same expectations as Bama fans. I *expect* them to prevail, no matter what.

McCarron's pass attempt on first down falls incomplete.

Yeldon rushes for 9 yards to the Bama 38 on second down. Seven seconds left as Bama uses its final time-out.

Here comes the Hail Mary pass, I say to myself. McCarron to History.

Instead, Bama calls another draw play to Yeldon, who runs 24 yards before cornerback Chris Davis knocks him out of bounds. I look at the game clock: 00:00. Overtime.

But wait—the replay officials want another look. When they're done looking, they add a single second to the game clock. That's all McCarron will need to toss a jump ball to Cooper in the end zone and we can all go home and say we have seen one of the great Bama comebacks. McCarron will win the Heisman. Auburn can say it had put the fear of God in Bama. The universe will settle back into alignment.

Saban has other ideas. He sends out his field goal unit, but this time without Foster in the lineup. Instead, the senior has been replaced by redshirt freshman Adam Griffith, who has a grand total of one made kick the entire season, a 20-yarder. And now, for the third kick of his Alabama career, he is going to try a 57-yarder with the Iron Bowl, the regular season and a BCS Championship appearance on the line? Huh?

I don't care how many 60-yarders he had made in practice. I don't care that he made a 32-yarder to win his high school state championship. This attempt is going to be from 25 yards farther away and against SEC players. This is going to be the kind of pressure that can destroy self-esteem, make your knees clatter like toy monkey cymbals. This is the Iron Bowl.

And by the way, if Saban thinks so much of Griffith, why didn't he have him attempt the shorter 30-yarder earlier in the quarter?

Saban is playing the percentages. According to the number crunchers at ESPN Stats & Info, the typical Hail Mary play has worked just 2 percent of the time for the trailing team over the last ten seasons. I know the game is tied, but you get the point: there's a reason why it's called a "Hail Mary." A last-second field goal attempt works about 28 percent of the time.

You know what happens next. Everyone knows what happens next. We've seen the highlight a million times—and that's just in the first hour after the game.

Griffith misses. Davis, the same guy who had knocked Yeldon out of bounds with one second remaining, catches the just-short field goal attempt deep in his own end zone and doesn't stop running until he reaches Bama's end zone 109 yards away.

"Is someone going to tackle this guy?" I hear myself say out loud.

Tackle him? Alabama barely *touches* him during the fourteen-second run. Field goal units aren't built for kickoff coverage. Or as CBS's Danielson says during a replay of the TD: "There are no athletes on the field for Alabama; they got all fat guys." (The *Wall Street Journal* later calculated that the average weight of Bama's blockers on the field goal unit was 289 pounds—about 70 pounds heavier per player than the Tide's punt coverage team.)

Davis ran past all of Bama's lumbering pursuers, marking only the fourth time in FBS (Football Bowl Subdivision) history that a missed field goal has been returned for a score. At some point, I just start laughing at the absurdity of it all.

Auburn has won. In fact, I have to do a double take at the scoreboard—yes, Auburn has won, thanks to the greatest ending in college football history. The Team of Destiny has beaten the Team of Dynasty.

The roar from the crowd has a concussive effect. It is heard from "the Loveliest Village" to 971 miles away in Columbus, Ohio. Fans pour onto the field like water from a ruptured dam. My buddy Thamel sees an elderly couple slowly make their way onto the turf and then celebrate with a quick kiss. He sees people stuff fists full of grass into their handbags and back pockets. He sees an entire family pose for a photo with the scoreboard in the background. They are going to use it for their Christmas cards.

You can see the disbelief and joy on the faces of the Auburn fans. You can see the disbelief and shock on the faces of the Bama fans. Auburn 34, Alabama 28 . . . and on Bo Jackson's birthday, too.

For a fourth consecutive week, a top-five BCS team loses a game. Never did I think that team would be Bama. Even Justin Timberlake can't believe what has just happened. He tweets: "That is one of THE BEST football games I've ever seen. What a wild ending!!"

With the loss, Saban's legacy gained a humbling new chapter. First of all, each of his key decisions backfired. You could argue that they backfired because his players didn't perform properly, and there would be some truth to that. Alabama's special teams were a disaster that day—a blocked punt, four missed field goals (at that point, the most missed field goals by an FBS team in 2013; and the most missed field goals by Bama since 2011) and Davis's 100-plus-yard TD return. Bama's defense gave up 296 rushing yards and saw Auburn convert eight of fifteen third-down plays. Bama's offense converted just three of six red zone chances. And six penalties, some of them crucial in nature, were killers.

Still, Alabama had 218 rushing yards of its own, passed for 277 yards, won the turnover and time-of-possession battle, and had more sacks than Auburn. And despite its mistakes, the Tide still had had a chance to win.

But Saban picked the wrong game to have a bad coaching day. In fact, November was becoming a bad month for Saban. Since 2010, his record against FBS opponents in August, September and October was a combined 31-1. His record in November was 7-5. He was now 0-6 against Auburn teams with nine or more victories.

"First time I ever lost a game that way," said Saban afterward. "First time I have ever *seen* a game lost that way."

The whole thing reminded me of 1980, when Bama was 7-0 and trying to win its third consecutive national championship. It was playing Mississippi State in Jackson, Missisippi, in early November.

Bama was ranked No. 1, had won twenty-eight games in a row and had beaten Mississippi State twenty-two consecutive times. With twenty-five seconds left to play, the Tide trailed by a field goal, but had first and goal at the Bulldogs' 4-yard line.

I was standing on the sidelines, just ten yards away from Bear Bryant and his offensive coordinator and future Bama athletic director Mal Moore, as the clock ticked down. Moore was talking to Bryant, but Bryant seemed hesitant to make a decision.

Quarterback Don Jacobs glanced at the sidelines, settled under the center, took the snap and was almost immediately hit as he moved right to run something from Bama's wishbone offense. The ball squirted out for Bama's fourth fumble of the day. Mississippi State recovered with six seconds remaining.

The game was over, and so was Bryant's dynasty. He would retire two seasons later and pass away shortly after his final game. Bama wouldn't win another national championship until 1992.

Byrant had been on his way to a three-peat, but lost. Saban had been even closer but met the same fate. At the time, I was convinced Saban had not only surpassed Bryant as the greatest coach in Alabama history, but was on the brink of becoming the greatest coach in college football history.

The loss to Auburn changed all that. I know it was just one game, but it was THE game. So much was at stake, and Saban stumbled. By missing that moment . . . that opportunity, Bama's dynasty was done, and in my mind Saban and Bryant were tied again.

Bama needed twelve years and three head coaches after Bryant before it won its next national title. Will it take that long for the Tide to return to glory? Probably not, but who knows how much longer Saban is going to coach. If anyone can fix what was broken, it's Saban. But is he going to be at Bama in five years? Three years? One year?

That's why Auburn's victory was so historic. It ended a dynasty. I criticized Saban for his game management against the Tigers, but I always genuflect over what he has accomplished during his tenure at Bama. I'll say it until the day I die: Do you know how hard it is to win a game in the SEC? Do you know how hard it is to reach a national championship game? To win one of them?

When I got home to Birmingham late that night, my wife asked me if I was upset about the Bama loss. After all, it had ended the Tide's chances at a first-ever three-peat.

But it didn't bother me. I truly appreciated the moment. There are different types of football history. That night at Jordan-Hare, I witnessed the end of a dynasty, but the beginning of a Malzahn legacy. I saw the greatest finish in college football history—better than Doug Flutie's Hail Mary pass against Miami in 1984, "The Play" in the 1982 Cal-Stanford game, the Bluegrass Miracle between LSU and Kentucky in 2002, the missed 2-point Nebraska conversion against Miami in 1984, or the Statue of Liberty play Boise State used in overtime to beat Oklahoma in 2007.

After Mississippi State beat Bama in 1980, bumper stickers appeared around Starkville. They read: "I Was There When We Beat The Bear."

Well, I was there when Auburn beat the great Saban and stopped the Bama national title streak at two. I was there when college football proved once again that there are no sure things.

In retrospect, I'm convinced the Auburn upset of Bama wouldn't have happened had the Tigers lost to Georgia. I think they would have crashed and burned against Bama. Instead, the Georgia win gave Auburn hope. And it gave us one of the best sports stories in decades.

I woke up at 5:30 Sunday morning and already had three calls from ESPN. Could I be in a local studio by 7:20 for a *SportsCenter* hit?

By then, Auburn athletic director Jay Jacobs had begun his campaign to bump a one-loss Auburn team over undefeated Ohio State in the BCS Standings.

"It's inarguable," said Jacobs. "It would be, quite frankly, un-American for us not to get a chance to go to Pasadena if we're able to beat Missouri [in the SEC Championship], and I believe the same about Missouri."

I agreed with Jacobs about Auburn jumping Ohio State—and said so on *SportsCenter*. It *was* inarguable. Auburn's nonconference and SEC schedule was much tougher than Ohio State's nonconference and Big Ten schedule. Auburn had just beaten the No. 1 team in the country. Ohio State hadn't beaten a team ranked in the top fifteen during the entire regular season. Auburn had beaten two of them.

I gave Urban Meyer credit for leading the Buckeyes to a second consecutive undefeated regular season (they still had the Big Ten Championship to play against Michigan State), but now there was no debate: Auburn (and maybe Mizzou as well) was the better team. In fact, I said I wouldn't pick against Auburn if it were playing the Denver Broncos. According to ESPN statisticians, the Tigers had won three games in 2013 in which their win probability was less than 10 percent (9 percent vs. Texas A&M, 7 percent vs. Georgia, 5 percent vs. Alabama).

To choose against destiny's darling would be, well, un-American.

Got married November first. He's a BAM. I'm Auburn.
The BAMs call us "Burners," for Auburners . . . hayseeds. I'm
proud to be a "Burner." I like hay. I like rolling around in the
hay. If Auburn would've lost the Iron Bowl, I would not be
in this truck with my husband. He would not be in the
truck with me. He might have been in here, but he would
have a few knots on his head.

—TAMMY

CHAPTER 18

The Aftermath

Saturday, December 7, 2013

Atlanta, Georgia

THE SEASON SKINNY: The rumors of Mack Brown's resignation reach critical mass. . . . Alabama drops to No. 4 in the BCS Standings and loses its death grip on first place in the AP poll for the first time since January 8, 2013. . . . Domino effect: two days after USC's rivalry loss to UCLA, Trojans AD Pat Haden hires Washington's Steve Sarkisian. An "outraged" Ed Orgeron immediately resigns, and Clay Helton is named interim coach for USC's bowl game. That means four different head coaches in less than three months.

Has it already been a week since "Kick Bama Kick"? Can't be. My eardrums are still in intensive care after the din of the Iron Bowl, and from the record-breaking number of callers who have jammed our phone lines since we went on the air Monday.

The Monday after an Alabama loss, especially an Alabama Iron Bowl loss, is always one of the most anticipated days for our show. We get the Bama fans in mourning, the Bama fans in denial and the Bama fans in outrage. Everyone else—Auburn fans, the LSU fans, the Ole Miss fans, the A&M fans, the Tennessee fans, the anti-Saban fans, even the Ohio State fans this time—gloats and revels in the Bama fans' misery.

"Tuscalosers" is what they're calling the Crimson Tide.

Bama fans were beside themselves when the Tide lost at South Carolina in 2010. And when they lost at home against Texas A&M in 2012, even Alabama goevrnor Robert Bentley, a Bama alum, came on the show to criticize Saban's play-calling in the final minutes of the game.

This time the Bama fans have been all over the map. They want to talk about the 109-yard field goal return, and about Saban's decision to attempt the last-second field goal. They want to defend Cade Foster, who has been the target of assorted idiotic Twitter messages rooting for his death.

Most of all, they want to vent. They want to blame. They simply can't believe Bama has been eliminated from the SEC race and, for all intents and purposes, the BCS race. So they take it out on me.

There's Larry, a sixty-eight-year-old retired policeman who calls the show and says, "How come you say Nick Saban blew the Iron Bowl? I thought you were a Roll Tide guy. You're just a Paul Finebaum fan. You're not an Alabama fan . . . We're still going to finish ahead of Auburn in the polls."

Larry has already determined that Alabama is going to beat Oklahoma in the Sugar Bowl and that Auburn is going to lose to Florida State in the BCS Championship. According to Larry's calculations, Bama will finish No. 2 in the country.

"That's a big accomplishment," Larry says.

"No it isn't," I say.

Auburn is going to play in the national title game. *That* is a big accomplishment. Bama is going to play on the undercard. If you're a Tide fan not named Larry, *that* is a big letdown.

During the course of the week, I've noticed a trend from the Bama callers: very few of them are openly criticizing Saban for his Iron Bowl decisions. It's as if they're scared of making him angry, scared that he'll somehow hear their criticisms and leave Bama for another job.

Meanwhile, all sorts of cool factoids are pouring in:

- During the Iron Bowl, 82 percent of the televisions in Birmingham had been tuned to the game.
- Chris Davis had received a standing ovation from his Auburn classmates when he walked into his Monday morning geology class.

- After Carolina defeated Tampa Bay the day after the Iron Bowl, Panthers quarterback Cam Newton took time in his postgame press conference to say, "War Eagle. War Eagle. War Damn Eagle."

- At the Birmingham airport, the Alabama T-shirts and hats that usually got preferential display in the gift shops had been moved aside for Auburn gear.

- The bookmakers in Vegas had decided that should the two teams meet in the BCS Championship, Ohio State would be a 2½-point favorite over Auburn. Of course, these were the same Vegas odds-makers who had made Bama a 10½-point favorite over War Damn Eagle.

- There were at least fourteen people, according to a Vegas sports-book director, who had purchased betting tickets earlier in the year giving them 1,000/1 odds that Auburn would win it all. At least one other person held a betting ticket giving him 500/1 odds. It had been purchased not long after the 2012 season had ended. The payoff for that one: $50,000.

- Malzahn had cashed his own winning contract ticket, thanks to a clause that paid him $25,000 for reaching eleven victories and another $100,000 for reaching the SEC Championship.

- The most famous football in Auburn history—maybe college football history—was missing.

I supported Auburn's lobbying campaign for the BCS National Championship, but I wasn't militant about it on my show. The undefeated winner of the Big Ten, which looks like it will be Ohio State, can also make a legitimate case for the national title game over the one-loss winner of the SEC.

But first Ohio State has to finish the season undefeated, and to do that the Buckeyes have to beat a sneaky-good Michigan State team. I don't think an Ohio State win is a foregone conclusion.

The debate caught the attention of Keith Olbermann, who invited me on his show a few nights ago to discuss the "Who's No. 2?" controversy. When Olbermann, a longtime favorite of mine, extends an invitation, you don't say no. For me, it is a bucket list moment, the sports equivalent of being on *Nightline* with Ted Koppel back in its glory years.

The interview was at 11:15 p.m. After a long season, I've given up on trying to be witty. For the Olbermann appearance, I decided I'd settle for trying to be informative—and to not nod off during commercial breaks. I admit it: I'm dragging a little bit these days. I've been traveling at least once and often twice a week. I've been doing my radio show five times a week. I've become a regular of sorts on *SportsCenter* and *College Football Live*, I'm doing *GameDay*. And I'm loving every minute of it. But like a true freshman playing on the varsity, I've hit the wall.

Olbermann asked me about the possibility of Duke beating FSU and Ohio State falling to Sparty, which would mean Iron Bowl II.

"At my age," I said, "that's simply the greatest fantasy I have left in my life."

Maybe I should be tired more often. Olbermann turned to the camera and said, "One of the great lines I've ever heard on ESPN—on any network, radio or television operation anywhere."

But I had meant it. The rest of the country might hate the possibility of a Bama-Auburn rematch, but I can't think of a more compelling story line. Can you imagine the hype? Can you imagine if Auburn won a national championship by beating Saban twice in the same season?

As if the Ohio State–Auburn debate isn't controversial enough, the state attorney in Tallahassee announced on Thursday that FSU quarterback and Heisman favorite Jameis Winston wouldn't be charged with felony sexual assault in connection with a criminal case filed by a woman in December 2012. In short, the state attorney for the Second Judicial Circuit decided after a three-week investigation that the evidence wasn't strong enough to support the likelihood of a conviction.

The decision isn't a surprise to me. The longer State Attorney Willie Meggs had taken to assess the winability of the case, the more I became convinced that charges wouldn't be brought. In the end, I wasn't impressed with Meggs or with Winston's attorney, Tim Jansen. Their performances on the day of the announcement were embarrassing. The grandstanding Meggs laughed during parts of his news conference. Jansen later suggested in his news conference the possibility that Winston had been "targeted" by women. Let me put it this way: if Meggs or Jansen ran for county dogcatcher, I wouldn't vote for either.

From a football standpoint, the decision allows Winston to continue his season with the undefeated Seminoles. Had he been charged with a felony, FSU policy would have dictated his immediate suspension.

The games that matter today are staggered: Mizzou vs. Auburn in the SEC Championship at 4 p.m. Eastern, followed by Duke vs. Winston's Florida State team in the ACC Championship at 8 p.m., followed by Ohio State vs. Michigan State in the Big Ten Championship at 8:17 p.m.

If FSU and Ohio State win, it will be the Noles and Buckeyes in the BCS Championship Game. If FSU or Ohio State loses, then the SEC champion will squeeze into the BCS Championship. And if FSU and Ohio State both lose, then suddenly Alabama is miraculously alive and well.

But before any of this unfolds, I first have to make a monumental fool of myself on national television.

I'm in Atlanta for the SEC Championship, while the *GameDay* show is in Indianapolis for the Big Ten Championship. So earlier this morning I was told to report to the Georgia Dome, where a camera crew and producer were waiting for me on the field for my remote shot with Chris Fowler back on the *GameDay* set.

I've done hundreds of these kinds of interviews over the years. But I've never done one just as the Auburn University Marching Band, all 375 members, commences its morning rehearsal by blasting away on trombones, tubas, snare drums, flutes, trumpets, cymbals and, for all I know, air horns at the exact moment I'm supposed to stare into a TV camera and start talking.

I saw the red light on the camera, but the band noise overwhelmed my earpiece and drowned out Fowler's question to me about Ohio State. So I panicked. Instead of cupping my hand over my non-earpieced left ear, or asking Chris to repeat the question, I stuck my finger in my left ear—and I mean *way* in. It was the only way I could sort of hear what Fowler was saying.

I started to explain to our national audience why I thought Ohio State was overrated. And I did it with a finger stuck halfway down my ear. I looked like Wile E. Coyote waiting for a stick of dynamite to explode.

Meanwhile, the Auburn band kept blaring away. So I kept my finger in my ear, and did so with my elbow pointed straight out.

A few minutes later (it seemed like hours), the interview was mercifully over. It was another lesson in the difference between doing TV and doing radio. In radio, the Auburn Marching Band doesn't play its halftime show in my studio. In TV, anything can happen—and did this morning.

Afterward, I checked my phone. There was a text message from the longtime senior coordinating producer of *GameDay*, Lee Fitting. Fitting has been a regular guest on my show throughout the season.

You have to understand that producing a three-hour live show is like walking a tightrope over a river gorge while someone is trying to tickle your feet. During the course of the season, I've stood at the back of the ESPN production truck studio while Fitting and his crew choreographed a show. Decisions are made on the fly. Orders are issued. It is a television ballet done in a phone booth, beholden to the images on the monitors and the second hand on a digital clock. It is not, generally speaking, a place where people yuk it up.

But according to those in the production truck this morning in Indianapolis, Fitting laughed so hard that he could barely breathe.

Others in the production truck later e-mailed to ask if I had suffered permanent ear canal or even brain damage, given how far my finger was poked in there. And when the camera cut from me in the Georgia Dome and back to the fellas on the *GameDay* set, they all had their fingers stuck in *their* ears.

I laughed too. What else are you going to do?

As the games play out, it becomes obvious that Auburn is a cut above Mizzou—and that both teams are a cut above Ohio State.

Poor Missouri. It scores 42 points and gains 534 total yards. Its quarterback, James Franklin, throws for 303 yards and three touchdowns, while the rushing attack gains 231 yards. And Mizzou still loses. By 17 points.

I almost feel sorry for Missouri's players. They never had a chance, because their coaches didn't have a clue how to stop Auburn's offense. If they did, Auburn wouldn't have scored 59 points and gained 677 total yards. Auburn running back Tre Mason wouldn't have gained 304 yards. Nick Marshall wouldn't have completed nine of eleven passes.

Of Auburn's eight touchdowns, seven of them are on rushing plays. Mason carries the ball forty-six times. I'm no football coach, but Mizzou's staff had zero answers after a week's worth of preparation.

Despite Auburn's convincing win, it still needs help. Ohio State or FSU will have to lose. And I have a better chance of growing a full head of hair than Duke has of upsetting the Seminoles.

So what happens? Duke and Florida State end the first quarter in a scoreless tie. Michigan State takes a 3–0 first-quarter lead over Ohio State. I can't believe what I'm seeing. We're going to get double upsets? We're going to get Iron Bowl II?

No, we're not.

The Seminoles score 45 consecutive points to win, 45–7. Winston is so unglued by the legal events of the week that he throws for only 330 yards and three touchdowns and runs for another.

With the FSU victory, Alabama is officially eliminated from the BCS conversation. But Auburn is very much alive.

Despite its underdog status, Sparty isn't backing down to the Buckeyes. Michigan State has a 17–0 lead but blows it. Then it trails by 7 late in the third quarter, but scores 17 straight points for a 34–24 victory.

Ohio State is out. Auburn is in.

Here we go again. The SEC is going for the eight-peat.

Ah, vindication. Everyone outside the conference has been trashing the SEC. They've been rooting for Ohio State not because they necessarily thought the Buckeyes were one of the two best teams in the country, but because they didn't want an SEC team in the BCS Championship. Then, boom, Michigan State puts the game away with a touchdown run with 2:16 left.

After the Buckeyes' loss, Urban Meyer detractors in general and SEC fans in particular (especially those from Florida) reveled in his failure.

Say what you want about him—and I know Gator fans won't forgive him for leaving UF—but the guy coached Ohio State to twenty-four consecutive victories. He beat rival Michigan twice in two years and he almost led a flawed Buckeyes team to the national championship game. Had they gotten there, Florida State would have destroyed them, but that's not the point.

Meyer is the second-best coach in the country. There's Saban, and then there's Meyer. Case closed.

Now that the regular-season and conference championship games are done, it's time to fill out my Heisman ballot. It doesn't take long. My ballot: 1—FSU's Winston; 2—Auburn's Mason; 3—Boston College running back Andre Williams.

The Heisman Trust sent out the ballots in late November, but I always wait until the last day to vote. I've never understood why any voter would submit his or her ballot before the conference championship games are played. And how could you vote early this year, especially when the state attorney didn't decide Winston's legal fate until only a few days ago?

I still have questions about the case—and always will. But those questions don't outweigh the reality of the situation, which is this: Winston wasn't charged. Once that legal situation was clarified (and his eligibility remained unaffected), I couldn't ignore another reality: he is the best college player in the country. So he gets my vote.

A few weeks earlier, Bama's McCarron would have been on my final-three Heisman list. Had he led the Tide to a win against Auburn and then a win against Missouri, he might have been atop that list. But given what Mason has done down the stretch, and what Williams has done all season for a very ordinary Boston College team, I don't have room for McCarron on my ballot.

A week later it becomes official: Winston wins in a landslide. No surprise there. McCarron finishes second and Northern Illinois quarterback Jordan Lynch finishes third. I'm happy for McCarron, but let's face it, hardly anybody but Heisman geeks and the immediate family of the finalists remembers who finishes second and third. That's just the nature of the award.

It has been an awful two weeks for Bama fans. They've seen the Tide lose the Iron Bowl, Auburn win the SEC Championship, FSU eliminate Bama from the BCS equation with the win against Duke, Michigan State upset Ohio State—which puts Auburn in the national title game—and McCarron lose his chance at a Heisman.

Listening to the Bama callers in mid-December, I can tell the chain of events has finally gotten to them. They were numb after the Iron Bowl loss, but can no longer ignore an awful (for them) truth: their arch-rival Auburn is now in position to win its second national title in four years—the same number of times as Bama during that period.

There is a faction of Bama fans who can't bring themselves to root for Auburn in the BCS Championship. It just hurts too much. They can't bear the thought of having to watch the Tigers receive the BCS crystal trophy, or listening to them gloat about another national championship.

There is also a part of them that wants Auburn to lose so they can blame the Tigers for ending the SEC national title win streak.

I take the broader view. If Auburn beats Florida State and Alabama beats Oklahoma in the Sugar Bowl, the SEC can finish 1-2 in the final poll. And as crazy as it sounds, I think Bama might still be the best team in the country.

There is one thing that Bama, Auburn and all SEC fans can agree on: Malzahn is a growing coaching force—not by the strength of his personality (understated), but by the strength of innovation and self-belief. This is a guy who dreamed big, even when he was a lowly assistant coach at little Hughes (Arkansas) High School (the football program has since been disbanded).

Malzahn used to cut and water the grass on the practice field. He used to wash uniforms and line the field. He was making what the Auburn Athletics Department spends on toothpaste. He lived in a trailer with his family.

But when a buddy asked him if he could see himself as an assistant coach at Arkansas, or Florida or Auburn, Malzahn said, "I wanna be the *head* coach." When his buddy asked him if he'd one day like to coach the Dallas Cowboys (Malzahn's favorite team), Malzahn said, "No, I want to *own* the Cowboys."

This is the guy who once told a fellow coach that he was going to "revolutionize" high school football in Arkansas. And he did, by creating an offense that was built around play volume. The more plays he could run, the more likely the opposing defenses would wear down. By speeding up the game, Malzahn exhausted his opponents, created instant mismatches (opposing coaches couldn't substitute fast enough) and increased his team's scoring chances. He won three state championships using that offense. Now he is doing the same thing in college football.

Going into the season, I didn't know much about Malzahn. We had shared a private plane for a charity event in Mobile. Bama defensive coordinator Kirby Smart was on that same plane.

Smart looked and sounded the part of a future head coach. Malzahn didn't have that same kind of charisma; he didn't knock either of my socks off. It was actually kind of awkward on the plane: Malzahn wasn't interested in polite small talk.

But the man can coach, and I have become a big fan. Whatever he lacks as far as a public persona has easily been outweighed by his football IQ, his organizational skills and his ability to communicate with his players. You don't turn a program around in one season just because of Xs and Os. There is more to it than that. You can have a great offensive scheme, but it means nothing unless you can convince your players to go all in.

Malzahn has stopped Alabama's momentum, and Auburn fans love him for that. Those feelings won't change, no matter what happens against FSU in the title game.

With this latest success, it is as if the Chizik Era never existed. I've never seen anything like it, where as time has passed more and more credit is given to the quarterback (Cam Newton) and offensive coordinator (Malzahn) than to the poor guy who coached the team (Chizik).

Chizik left a footprint, but he left it in sand. Now it is being mostly erased in a short period of time. Nobody dislikes him per se; they just don't consider him a key figure in the Auburn football time line.

Maybe they would feel differently if he had found the game-winning ball from the Iron Bowl. Turns out that Chris Davis had dropped the ball after crossing the goal line. In the madness and mayhem of the touchdown celebration, nobody saw a ball boy retrieve it.

Unlike the balls used by Auburn, the one kicked by Alabama didn't have a school logo on it. It took a few days to sort everything out, but the

Bama-owned ball is now in possession of Auburn (a Bama spokesperson essentially said the school isn't in a hurry to ever see the ball again).

A memorabilia expert placed the value of the ball at $50,000 . . . $100,000 if Auburn beats Florida State.

The memorabilia expert obviously didn't attend Auburn. If he had, he'd know the value of that particular pigskin is priceless.

If you're not ticking them off, you're not doing something right.

—JIM FROM TUSCALOOSA

CHAPTER 19

A Worthy Ending to a Worthy Season

Monday, January 6, 2014
Pasadena, California

THE SEASON SKINNY: The video of an Alabama woman leaping over people in the Superdome to try to slug an Oklahoma fan surfaces on YouTube and goes viral. . . . In other bowl news: Johnny Football ends his college career with five touchdown passes in a comeback win against Duke in the Chick-fil-A Bowl, and Michigan State beats Stanford in the hundredth Rose Bowl, breaking a nine-game Big Ten losing streak in the granddaddy of them all.

The Paul Finebaum "I'm Wrong About Everything Mea Culpa Tour" continues. Or as heavyweight champion Evander Holyfield once said to a cowering Charley Steiner, one of the *SportsCenter* anchors from the 1990s, in one of the show's famous ads: "Charley, c'mon out and get your whuppin'!"

In this remake, I am Charley and Oklahoma coach Bob Stoops is Holyfield. In my defense, I'm not cowering under a desk.

On January 2, the same day as the Sugar Bowl matchup between Oklahoma and Alabama, I had appeared on *SportsCenter* and said that Stoops and the Sooners were in for another embarrassing loss. I criticized Stoops for some of his previous anti-SEC remarks and reminded everyone that OU had lost to a Texas program in disarray.

So, of course, Oklahoma took Bama apart like a Lego building, 45–31.

If you're going to dish it out, you also have to be willing to take the heat, so I made another *SportsCenter* appearance the day after the OU win. Chris McKendry did the interview from the Bristol studios and, sure enough, they rolled the tape of my Bama-OU prediction.

When she asked for my reaction, I said, "There's nothing to say other than I'm an idiot."

Looking back, I wish I would have known what Saban soon realized about his team the night of the Sugar Bowl: Oklahoma's players were much more focused than Alabama's players.

I wish I would have known that Saban, for all of his coaching skills, simply couldn't get through to his players as the season had worn on. He had begun to lose them after the Tide's impressive performance against LSU. That's when the players began to feel invincible, and stopped bothering to listen to Saban and the other coaches. Looking back, that attitude helped explain the sluggish win against Mississippi State, the loss to Auburn and the beat-down by Oklahoma.

I wish I would have known that some of those Tide players had treated the Sugar Bowl as a consolation game—were more interested in collecting their bowl swag than they were in beating OU.

Oklahoma hadn't played that way. The Sooners had played with purpose, with a chip on their shoulder pads. Stoops and OU had a point to prove to people like me—and all those who had assumed Bama would roll over Oklahoma—and they proved it.

Some of the Bama players felt entitled. They had assumed that since they were the Crimson Tide, winners of back-to-back BCS Championships, success was their divine right by virtue of their letter of intent. They had forgotten what it took to win those championships. Even AJ McCarron later admitted as much: that some of the younger players on the Bama roster never fully bought into the Tide's culture and mission. And nothing Saban did or said could shake them out of their stupor.

Part of that was Saban's responsibility: he couldn't—or didn't—prevent the meltdown. Part of it was the players' fault. For whatever reason, they had tuned out one of the best coaches in the history of the game. Or as McCarron would tell CBS Sports's Jim Rome: "Success was our killer." An 11-0 start had ended with an 0-2 finish.

Saban arrived in Pasadena a few days ago to be part of the ESPN coverage team. He is joined by Tim Tebow, the newly hired analyst for the SEC Network. Whenever they talk in the production meetings about matchups, about handling the BCS Championship circus, about the challenges Malzahn and Jimbo Fisher face, about the mind-set of Winston, about, well, anything, I listen.

The gist of their lessons is this:

- It is difficult to carry momentum into the bowl season. But Fisher, a former Saban assistant coach, is using Saban's past BCS Championship preparation schedules as a template for Florida State's bowl schedule.
- Auburn's maligned defense, especially its front four, is good enough to create problems for FSU and Winston.
- The weight of a Heisman and the expectations that come with that trophy could affect Winston's play in the game. How he deals with those expectations will be a key factor, as will his ability to deal with different coverages.
- For all the deserved talk about Malzahn's play-calling ability, Fisher is one of the best coaches at picking the right play at the right moment.
- FSU will create more mismatches than Auburn.
- Auburn will have to score at least 35 points to have a chance to win.

My BCS Championship day begins at 5:45 a.m. That's when I walk into the TV compound at the Rose Bowl. The only person in the production trailer: Tebow. On my list of surreal work experiences, eating a bowl of Cinnamon Toast Crunch while Tebow talks football is right up there with talking movies with Bill Murray. Tebow didn't do much in his college career other than win a Heisman in 2007, lead Florida to a BCS Championship in 2008 and earn a title ring as a backup on the Gators' 2006 BCS Championship team. In fact, it was that 2006 Florida team that began the SEC national title win streak.

We do our assorted TV hits and I pick Auburn to win, 31–27. I believe in destiny, in Malzahn's offense, in the possibility of FSU stage fright. I believe that Florida State wouldn't be in the national title game had it played Florida's SEC schedule (at LSU, at Missouri, Georgia in Jacksonville, Vandy, at South Carolina, among others) or Tennessee's schedule (a nonconference trip to Oregon and a stretch of SEC opponents that featured Florida, Georgia, South Carolina, Alabama, Missouri, Auburn and Vandy). I believe Auburn's defense is better than people think, and that Florida State's offense isn't as good as the statistics said they are. I believe in the Bo Jackson–sized chip on Auburn's shoulder.

Back in July, the oddsmakers had said the over/under on Auburn wins was 6½. The Tigers were 75/1 long shots to win the SEC. They were football nobodies to the smart guys then, and they are football nobodies to the waitress who took my order at an Italian restaurant in Pasadena two nights before the game.

"Who do you like in the game?" I said.

She thought about it for a moment. "I like Alabama," she said.

I didn't correct her. Even in Pasadena, where Auburn is playing one of the biggest games in its history, we are still living in Saban's world.

The once-deserted production trailer is filled with announcers, analysts, guest analysts, reporters, producers, directors, researchers and me. At one point I stand off to the side and realize we have two coaches in the room who have won a combined five national titles (Lou Holtz and Saban). We also have a mini–Heisman House, what with Desmond, Tebow and the just-arrived Johnny Manziel.

I had been tough on Manziel earlier in the season. But as the year has progressed and Johnny Football has upped his game and toned down his off-field hijinks, I have become a believer.

GameDay contributor George Whitfield, the quarterback guru who had worked with Manziel during the off-season, introduces me to Manziel in the trailer. I might as well wear a name tag that says "Hello, My Name is PAUL FINEBAUM . . . and I'm very sorry."

"Johnny, I owe you big-time," I say, explaining that without him there would have never been that September exchange with Drake on *SportsCenter.*

And then I tell him that my criticism of his off-field actions were made not because I disliked him, but because I thought he was disrespecting the game and his team.

"I said what I thought at the time," I tell him. "But you won me over."

Manziel nods and says he appreciates the explanation, but I'm not sure he cares what outsiders think of him. He laughs when I remind him about my waving a handkerchief in surrender during the *SportsCenter* encounter with his buddy Drake. He even mentions the chat I had with his dad back at College Station earlier in the season. Bottom line: he trusts his own instincts. If the rest of us don't like it, tough.

I watch the game first from the Rose Bowl press box and later from the sidelines, where I become an easy target for FSU fans angry over my Auburn pick. I can handle rude, but a mixture of $13 tall boy beers and all afternoon to drink them has turned parts of the FSU crowd into f-bombing idiots. I just shrug my shoulders and wish them good luck with their parole boards.

From the opening kickoff, it's fascinating to see the pregame observations of Tebow and Saban come to life.

They were right: it *is* difficult for Florida State to maintain the momentum from the regular season. The Seminoles are used to blowing teams out of games, but they are a shell of their regular-season selves in the early going.

Winston plays tight in the first quarter. Auburn is mixing up its coverages. The Tigers' defensive line is pressuring the Heisman winner, sacking him twice.

Auburn isn't tight. It has a 7–3 lead at the end of the quarter. Then a 14–3 lead. Then a 21–3 lead. And it could be 31–3 if Marshall doesn't underthrow a wide-open Ricardo Louis and Cody Parkey doesn't miss a 33-yard field goal.

Still, this game is on the verge of becoming a blowout. Florida State is reeling.

When FSU fails to convert a third and three with less than two minutes remaining in the half, I think Auburn is one more score from completely traumatizing the Seminoles. The Tigers have gouged FSU's run defense and found lots of soft spots in its secondary. Now they'll get the ball back with plenty of time to stick a stake in Florida State's heart.

Fisher must be thinking the same thing. Because he calls one of the most audacious plays at one of the most critical points of the game: a fake punt that catches Auburn by complete surprise. First down. Seven plays later, FSU cuts the lead to 21–10.

Remember what Tebow and Saban had said? *Fisher is a master play-caller.* Fisher's decision to run that fake punt will turn out to be the defining moment of the game.

The Seminoles are reenergized by the fake punt and the touchdown that follows. You can see it in their body language after the score. You can see it when they run to their locker room at halftime, and when they return for the third quarter. (Tebow tells me at halftime that he thinks the FSU players look slightly out of shape.)

I don't have kids, but if I did, I would tell them about the second half of the 2013 BCS Championship. First of all, the nervous, jittery Winston of the first half has been replaced in the second half by the composed prodigy who has wowed everyone all season long.

Auburn still pressures him, still sacks him, and FSU trails, 21–13, to start the final quarter of the final game of the season. But those Florida State mismatches that Saban and Tebow had talked about are becoming more obvious.

Winston needs just five plays to lead FSU to a touchdown early in the fourth quarter. Auburn 21, FSU 20.

The Tigers answer with a field goal. Auburn 24, FSU 20.

The Noles respond with a 100-yard kickoff return. FSU 27, Auburn 24.

Auburn answers with a 37-yard TD run by Mason. Auburn 31, FSU 27.

Only seventy-nine seconds remain in the game. The Auburn bench is going nuts. The Auburn fans are going nuts. I'm standing at field's edge with Manziel and Vanderbilt coach James Franklin (another ESPN guest analyst) when Mason scores to put the Tigers ahead—and even they are caught up in the moment.

I look at the scoreboard. I had hit my pregame prediction exactly on the number. Vindication. I had taken a million cheap shots for sticking with the Tigers, and now the 1,000/1 long shot looks like it is going to come through. Auburn just has to survive these final seventy-nine seconds.

It doesn't happen.

There is a reason why I voted for Winston to win the Heisman. And it is borne out on the final Florida State drive.

Starting at FSU's own 20, Winston moves the Seminoles down the field like it is a seven-on-seven drill. He completes six of seven passes. He is helped by a missed Auburn tackle early in the drive and a no-brainer Auburn pass interference call late in the drive. It is almost too easy when he finds the human mismatch, 6-foot-5, 234-pound FSU wide receiver Kelvin Benjamin, open in the end zone for the game-winning touchdown.

Auburn gets the ball back with nine seconds left, but it doesn't matter. The Tigers will receive no answer to their Pasadena Prayer.

FSU 34, Auburn 31.

That's when I think back to one of Saban's remarks:

Auburn will need to score at least 35 points to have a chance to win.

The SEC's national championship win streak has come to an end. And for the first time since 2008, the state of Alabama will have to make do without a new crystal trophy.

There isn't much to do except appreciate having been witness to a great game. The Seminoles overcame the largest deficit in BCS National Championship history. Winston completed only 11 of 25 for 120 yards during his first ten drives of the game, but when it mattered, in the final two FSU drives, he hit 9 of 10 for 117 yards.

The last time an SEC team lost a national championship, Winston was eleven years old.

As part of our postgame coverage, host Rece Davis and I are scheduled to do a TV hit on the field. As we wait for the set to be unfolded, Florida State fans let me have it. The nicest thing they chant is "A-C-C."

Yes, A-C-C. And if their conference wins six more consecutive national titles, they can chant "S-E-C."

But Florida State won fair and square. It had overcome a first-half lead that might have broken other teams' spirit. It had taken one of the great gambles in championship history by running a fake punt in its own territory. It had refused to fold even when Auburn took a last-minute lead. It deserved to hoist that crystal trophy.

So as the crew members ready the set, I walk over to the FSU fans and start doing the Florida State tomahawk chop as a way to make peace. I've been at the Rose Bowl all morning, all afternoon and all night. I'm a little loopy.

Some of the fans mother-f me, but most of them start doing the chop. Before long, I'm leading several thousand FSU fans in the chop . . . in the Rose Bowl . . . not long after the final BCS Championship Game. How cool is that?

When I take my place on the set with Rece, something strange happens. My eyes begin to water. I don't know why—maybe it's allergies—but I can't stop from tearing up. We are only a few minutes from air and I look like I've been crying because of the SEC loss. I can see the caption on Deadspin: "Paul Finebaum Sheds a Single Tear for the SEC."

Right before we go live, my tear ducts finally cooperate. The same can't be said for Auburn's Tre Mason, who did weep after the loss. It isn't official, but he had played his final game for Auburn. The immensely likeable running back is going to forgo his senior season of eligibility for the NFL Draft.

Mason had played magnificently. He had run for 195 yards, breaking Bo Jackson's single-season rushing record, with 1,816. (Jackson had spent time with Mason during the team's pregame meal, and had addressed the Auburn offense. They call it the "Auburn Family" for a reason.)

After nineteen-plus hours at the Rose Bowl, we finally leave the stadium, with a police escort and a pair of FSU fans still yelling at me.

In some ways, it feels like it's the last day of school, high school graduation. Despite fingers in my ears, verbal gaffes and apologies, right and wrong predictions, tens of thousands of miles flown and endless debates with our show's callers, I have survived long enough to get my diploma. I've come a long way since Shreveport, or doing radio shows at car washes.

I think about the irony and the symmetry of the 2013 season. It began with the much-hyped Alabama, and ended with the little-regarded Auburn. That's right, Auburn. Yes, Florida State had won the BCS Championship, but the 2013 season was as much about what Saban and the Crimson Tide didn't do—and what the Tigers almost did—as it was about the Seminoles and Jameis Winston.

I think about the what-ifs. What if Auburn hadn't taken a chance on Malzahn? There would have never been an "Immaculate Deflection," or a "Kick Bama Kick." There wouldn't have been an SEC Championship in 2013, a trip to the BCS Championship or a Rose Bowl scoreboard that had Auburn ahead with just seventy-nine seconds remaining on the clock.

I don't want to go all magical and mystical on you, but Malzahn had an unusual, almost unexplainable ability to lift his team. Can he do it again in 2014? I have no idea, but I guarantee you that this time no Vegas bettor is going to get 1,000/1 odds on the Tigers winning it all.

Can Florida State repeat in 2014? As long as Winston stays healthy and Clemson keeps losing games that matter in the three-team ACC (FSU, Clemson and new member Louisville), I don't see why the Seminoles can't at least reach the first-ever four-team College Football Playoff. But as Saban and Alabama have discovered, the championship math gets much harder when you go for the two-peat.

Can Bama become Bama again? Not if they don't find a replacement for McCarron. Not if Saban doesn't make staff changes. Not if the team quits like that again.

Can the SEC return to the national championship game? I don't see why not. At least eight of the league's teams are top-25 material: Auburn, LSU, Bama, South Carolina, Georgia, Texas A&M, Florida and Ole Miss. And don't be surprised if one of the remaining six teams comes out of nowhere.

Auburn can tell you all about that sort of thing.

Is the SEC still the best conference? You're damn right it is.

My buddy Bob Stoops likes to question the depth of the SEC. He says it's top-heavy.

Hmmm. According to ESPN Stats and Info, that supposedly top-heavy conference had ten teams with winning records in 2013. It finished 7-3 in its bowl games, which is as many wins as the combined totals of the Big Ten and the ACC, and four more than Stoops's Big 12.

The SEC finished with seven teams in the AP top 25 and four in the top seven. Only the Pac-12 came close to that figure.

Mississippi State finished fifth in the SEC West and won its bowl game by 37 points. Vandy finished fourth in the SEC East and won its bowl game by 17. LSU had lost Zach Mettenberger to a torn ACL and still won its bowl game by 7. Georgia was playing without an injured Aaron Murray and lost its bowl game by just 5 points to Nebraska.

South Carolina weathered quarterback and Clowney injuries throughout the season. Mizzou had quarterback injuries. Auburn didn't pick a starting quarterback until fall camp. And yet the Game-cocks beat Wisconsin in their bowl. Missouri beat Oklahoma State in its bowl. Auburn reached the national championship.

Depth? The SEC is deeper than the continental shelf.

I made my share of apologies in 2013, but I won't apologize for planting the SEC flag deep into the ground.

"It's been a hell of a run," the SEC's Slive told reporters after the game, his head held high.

Slive was talking about the end of the national title win streak. But he also could have been talking about my own last eight years surfing the barrel wave known as the SEC.

Slive was right, of course. It had been a hell of a run. For the SEC. And for me.

When can we start again?

What do I want the other conferences to know
about the SEC? The love and the passion. The coaches.
The way we do things. The way our players git after it.
Yeah, we get wild, we get crazy. Are they equal to the SEC?
They ain't nowhere equal to the SEC.

—TAMMY

Epilogue

Monday, May 20, 2014
Charlotte, North Carolina

THE OFF-SEASON SKINNY: According to the smart guys in Vegas, seven of the top fifteen favorites to win the first College Football Playoff are from the SEC. . . . ESPN.com's Mark Schlabach declares Alabama running back Derrick Henry as "the sport's next superstar." . . . I'm still waiting for my invitation to join the College Football Playoff's selection committee.

Things happen:

- **Remember those August 31, 2013, *GameDay* predictions about Alabama?**

    Desmond Howard had said a young SEC team could come along and shock everybody. Hello, Auburn.

    Herbstreit had said complacency could be Bama's undoing. He was right too—McCarron admitted in late January that the younger Tide players didn't buy into the team's mission.

    Coach Corso had said placekicking could be the difference in Bama's season. Hello, Auburn game.

- **Remember my August 31, 2013, *GameDay* prediction about Ohio State?**

    I had said that if the Buckeyes played in the SEC, they wouldn't finish higher than fifth or sixth in the league. As it turned out, four SEC teams finished ahead of Ohio State in the final rankings.

When the Bama players returned to work in January, they found a poster taped to each of their lockers. The poster featured the scores of Bama's loss in the Iron Bowl and the loss to OU in the Sugar Bowl. In the background were images of Oklahoma and Auburn players. In the foreground was a warning from Saban: "If You Continue to Do The Same Thing That You Have Always Done You Will Get the Same Result Guaranteed. 0-2."

■ **Bama got a new quarterback (Jameis Winston backup Jake Coker transferred from FSU and is eligible to play immediately), a new offensive coordinator (Kiffin) and a more focused Saban.**

■ **I was walking through a terminal at the Charlotte airport when someone yelled, "Hey, Paul!" I turned around and the guy had his finger in his ear, his elbow stuck out and a smile on his face. I've been getting that a lot lately.**

■ **Spurrier got a $700,000 raise, pushing his salary to $4 million.**

What he's done in the last three seasons is comparable to what he did at Florida. Spurrier hasn't won a national title as a Gamecock—yet—but South Carolina is a much more challenging gig than Florida. He has three top-ten finishes in a row and three bowl victories in a row. He has cemented his already brilliant football legacy even more.

■ **Malzahn got the Paul Bear Bryant Coach of the Year award. If you don't think that sends a chill up the spine of Bama fans, you need to reread this book.**

It was Malzahn's fifth national Coach of the Year honor. I'm still trying to figure out how he didn't win the Maxwell and Bobby Dodd

Coach of the Year awards too. Did those voters not notice his name on the ballots?

■ **Georgia got Florida State defensive coordinator Jeremy Pruitt. Of course, FSU got Pruitt from Alabama.**

"There's no doubt that [the SEC] is the best conference in the country, and I feel like the University of Georgia is the best school in the conference," Pruitt told reporters. "I wouldn't be here today if I didn't think so."

A reported $300,000-per-year raise helps too.

■ **Missouri defensive end Michael Sam, the co-SEC Defensive Player of the Year, announced that he was gay.**

First of all, I'm stunned the story stayed a secret for so long (his Mizzou coaches and teammates had known since last August).

Second, I'm in awe of the class and dignity exhibited by Sam, his Tiger teammates, Gary Pinkel and his coaching staff and the entire Mizzou family. Their approach to a delicate and challenging situation was pitch-perfect.

Several weeks after Sam's announcement, I found myself in Kansas City on a snowy winter day, speaking with a Mizzou alumni group. I witnessed firsthand the pride Tiger fans took in the school's approach, and the support and genuine love they had for Sam.

■ **Jadeveon Clowney, who finished the year with just three sacks and eleven and a half tackles for losses, declared for the NFL Draft. At the February NFL Combine, the 6-foot-5, 266-pound defensive end was a workout freak show, running a 4.53-second 40-yard dash. That's only slightly slower than what running backs Tre Mason of Auburn and De'Anthony Thomas ran (4.50) at the Combine, and was actually faster than Boston College's Andre Williams (4.56) and Ohio State's Carlos Hyde (4.66).**

I wish Clowney a long and successful NFL career. I also wish I had gone a little easier on him during the 2013 season. Still friends?

- **Manziel declared for the NFL Draft.**

  (See Clowney, above.)

  Manziel didn't throw at the Combine, and opinions among the draft experts about his NFL future were mixed. I've learned my lesson: I wouldn't bet against him.

- **Bobby Petrino was hired by Louisville after Charlie Strong took the Texas job. I told you Saban wasn't going to Texas.**

- **Texas was dead serious about trying to money-whip Saban.**

  Depending on whom you talk to—Bama big hitters or Texas big hitters—the Longhorns were prepared to give Saban somewhere between a $12 million and $15 million signing bonus and a salary package worth $100 million (plus performance bonuses).

- **James Franklin moved to Penn State.**

  I don't blame Bill O'Brien for leaving State College for the Houston Texans. I don't blame Franklin for leaving Vanderbilt for the land of We Are. The NFL is a step up from Penn State. Penn State is a step up from Vandy.

  Franklin did something in Nashville, Tennessee, that I didn't think was possible: he made Commodore football relevant. He proved you could win on a consistent basis there. He's one of the best and brightest coaches to come through the SEC in a long time.

  So maybe that's why I don't understand why somebody so bright would do something so coldhearted and dishonorable as Franklin did when he poached five of the recruits he had previously convinced to commit to Vanderbilt.

  Franklin isn't the first coach to switch jobs and then flip recruits from his old program. He won't be the last. But I guess I expected more than the dispassionate, boilerplate "I'm comfortable with what we did professionally" answer he gave me on the radio show when I asked him about poaching the Vandy recruits. There was no acknowl-edgment of how this would adversely affect the Vanderbilt program, no hint of regret.

Vanderbilt gave Franklin his first head coaching job, which Frank-lin used to get a better job. That's how it works. No one at Vandy be-grudged him the opportunity. In fact, shortly after Franklin left for Penn State, I spoke with the father of a Commodores team captain. The father raved about Franklin.

But that was before Franklin started flipping Vandy recruits. Now I wonder what the father would say.

Franklin could have left Nashville as a football hero, the classy coach who was different from the others. Instead, he fell victim to the pressures of recruiting. He compromised. He blew it.

■ **Stanford suffered a crushing de-commit after the season. Derek Mason, the Cardinal's defensive coordinator (excuse me—at Stanford they haughtily call it, "The Willie Shaw Director of Defense"), accepted the head coaching position at Vandy. Or as they call it in Nashville these days: "The Director of Kicking the Vols' Butts."**

Mason becomes the fifth African-American head coach in SEC his-tory (Franklin, Joker Phillips, Sumlin, Croom and Mason). Two of the five were Vandy hires.

■ **People outside the SEC keep telling me the SEC's reign is finished. I try not to do a spit take when they say these things.**

In a supposed "down" year, the SEC finished with three teams in the top five, four teams in the top ten and one team in the national champi-onship game. And did I mention how the SEC did in recruiting?

According to ESPN's Recruiting Nation rankings, seven of the top nine classes belong to SEC programs. Of the fifteen five-star recruits— the elite of the elite—ten of them signed with SEC schools. (Five of them signed with Alabama, which had the No. 1 recruiting class for the third consecutive year.) Fourteen of the top twenty recruits in the country decided to take their talents to the SEC.

Texas A&M's Sumlin said it best when describing the Aggies' 2014 recruiting effort: "We had a great year. The only problem is we were fourth in the country and third in our own division."

- **Butch Jones might be on to something at Tennessee.**

At least, his highly ranked incoming recruiting class seems to think so. I give him one more year, two tops, before the Vols are a national player again.

- **Muschamp made staff changes at Florida.**

If that doesn't work, the next to go will be Muschamp. The Gators lost their last seven games in 2013, missed a bowl for the first time since 1990, lost to Georgia for the third straight year and suffered their worst season in thirty-four years.

In my heart of hearts I think Muschamp is good enough to prove 2013 was an aberration. But if he doesn't turn it around in Year Four (and that means he can't lose to Georgia again), there won't be a Year Five.

- **Kentucky football still stinks, but perhaps there's hope. The Wildcats had 50,831 for their 2013 spring game. Great. They had 54,986 for their 2013 regular-season finale. Not so great. UK finished 2-10 overall and 0-8 in the SEC. But Mark Stoops actually beat Saban for a top national recruit. It helped that the recruit was from Kentucky, but still . . .**

Not to rub it in (OK, just a little bit), but not only did the SEC reach the BCS Championship in January, but two SEC teams (Kentucky and Florida) reached the NCAA Final Four.

As usual, it was an SEC players reunion at the NFL draft. Eleven SEC players were drafted in the first round of the 2014 draft (including my buddies Clowney at No. 1 and Manziel at No. 22), more than double the total of any other conference. And, as usual, the SEC led all conferences (for the eighth year in a row) with the most picks. Its 49 picks were more than the Big 10 and Big 12 combined.

- **Harvey Updyke still keeps in touch.**

  He lives in a state not called Alabama. He doesn't charge me Honey Buns to talk.

- **Alabama or Auburn will win the SEC in 2014 (I'm leaning toward Bama beating Auburn in the Iron Bowl), Florida will be the surprise team of the league.**

- **If Saban leaves Alabama, Kirby Smart won't be the first choice as his successor. I like Smart, but his stock value has depreciated.**

- **If you think Tennessee fans couldn't stand Kiffin when he ditched UT for USC, just wait if his play-calling helps Bama beat the Vols on his October 25 return to Knoxville.**

- **And one last thing: Charles from Reeltown called.**

  He said he was going to give me a country-boy ass whuppin'.
  I probably deserve it.

Acknowledgments

I t was during a commercial break that I realized I was about to become an author.

It was December 5, 2012, and I was doing the show at Sirius XM's Lincoln Center jazz studio when Pat Smith, who has run our show since the 1990s, forwarded me an e-mail from Lee Habeeb, a well-known political commentator. Habeeb was suggesting I hook up with his friend David Vigliano, a literary agent, during my New York visit. The only surprise was that it really wasn't that surprising. The previous day, Reeves Wiedman's long-awaited piece in the *New Yorker* (six months in the making) had come out and I didn't have to stand outside in Columbus Circle on this wintry December day to know which way the wind was blowing.

The next day I rushed to Vigliano's Park Avenue office after speaking at the IMG/*Sports Business Journal* conference in Times Square. I walked in, forty-five minutes late, and wasn't sure what to expect. Based on Vigliano's curriculum vitae—having represented clients whose books had hit No. 1 on the *New York Times* list fifteen times, from Pearl Jam to Rick Pitino to Pope John Paul II—I must say I was underwhelmed to be greeted by a dog. Not an impressive canine, but a pooch named Pepper, an Alaskan Klee Kai, who weighed less than a bagel and lox with a smear. Before I made it to Vigliano's office, her running buddy, Sunny, all twenty-seven pounds' worth, said hello. In search of my first book deal, I was suddenly looking for some Gravy Train to keep these two mongrels from nipping at my heels.

"I have a great idea for a book," barked Vigliano from the corner office.

Vigliano is a bear of a man with a soft, gentle smile. He had an idea for a book, and it involved me, college football and the SEC. Thus began this project.

I've always found this part of a book to be extremely tedious, something akin to the speech of the schlep who wins the Oscar for best set design. In other words, I really don't care who your first-grade teacher was back in Hoboken. However, there were many people who helped shape this project and I would probably lose some sleep if I didn't thank them properly.

The people behind the scenes don't get enough credit, but the aforementioned Pat Smith has been a critical part of the show for twenty-one years, and this project wouldn't have been possible without him. Kerry Adams, Dallas Downs, John Hayes, Ryan Haney and Alex Bell (who took the famed call from Harvey Updyke) are just a handful of the many who have been key players along the way.

I consulted many friends during the early days of this project who offered key advice, wonderful writers, authors and book people such as Lars Anderson, Bruce Feldman, Carla Baranauckas, Gene Hallman, Howell Raines, Warren St. John, Alex Berenson, Amy Gary, Rachel Bachman, Bob Carlton, Jake Reiss, Clyde Anderson and Colin Cowherd.

I've gotten to know too many lawyers, but close friends like Archbishop Joseph Marino, Tommy Limbaugh, Steve Cohen, Scott Greenstein, Russ Campbell, Mike Douglas, Joe Buffington, John Falkenberry, John Kosner, Lowell Singer, Steve Vecchione, Joe Tessitore, Walt Aldridge (with whom I cowrote my first country song), Bill Thomas, Larry Silverstein (my oldest friend from high school and college) and, more recently, Judd Harwood have managed to keep me in press boxes more often than civil court. And without Nick Khan of CAA, who watched over this project while he was trying to find me a real job, I doubt this book, or anything I've done lately, would have been possible. I will spend the rest of my career thanking Nick for taking a chance on me, and it still won't be enough.

I would be remiss if I didn't also thank Lee Fitting, the senior co-ordinating producer of ESPN's College *GameDay*, for providing me with the greatest thrill of my career this past fall, for allowing me to tag along with the most talented group of people on television, and for allowing me to play an infinitesimal role in the sport's greatest show. And many thanks to the Bear, Chris Fallica, for his friendship and help with this project, and to his wife, Molly, as well, who helps the trains run on time at *GameDay*.

From the Southeastern Conference, there has been no closer friend and mentor than Mike Slive. Not only is he the best commissioner in sports, he's like the older brother I never had (we share the same birthday). And if there were a middle brother, it would be his long-time friend and television consultant (and fellow booklover) Chuck Gerber.

Justin Connolly, my boss at the SEC Network, has been intricately involved in this project, as well as his boss, John Skipper, the president of ESPN, who took an early interest in this adventure and never wavered with his support, understanding and wise counsel.

Slive and I have a two-person "book club" that meets often for lunch and the exchange of books. We spend weeks scouring book stores for rare finds. On the day of my hiring at ESPN, Slive told me there had been a strange request from another person for entry in the coveted fraternity. I said sorry, but the membership was closed. No exceptions. Membership would remain at two. Then he told me John Skipper had inquired. Okay, so I made an exception.

The team at Harper has been fantastic, headed by David Hirshey, one of the truly iconic editors in the business. The many meals with

Hirshey and Brian Grogan, head of sales, have been unforgettable and ridiculously expensive. Shout-outs also to Barry Harbaugh, who is much too young to be this good of an editor, to Sydney Pierce, who is even younger, but showed grace under pressure in overseeing the photo insert, and to art director Milan Bozic, who helped supervise the cover shoot at Bryant-Denny Stadium.

Also, many thanks to Stephanie Druley and Gracie Blackburn of ESPN, both of whom have worked closely with the team at HarperCollins.

Danny Sheridan, the sports handicapper from Mobile and frequent radio guest, offered great advice along the way and was the first to lay odds this project would be a success. We will see soon if Danny has a rare miss when it comes to being on the mark. And Vince Thompson, one of my oldest and dearest friends in the world, kept his eagle eye on this project, and with his Atlanta-based team led by Michelle Grech and Grant Guffin, helped pull off the billion-to-one shot, getting the photo shoot in the upper deck at Bryant-Denny Stadium done in less than two hours and under (barely) $200,000.

On the personal side, Gene Wojciechowski has been so much fun to work with. I've only known him since 1978 and this is our first—and hopefully not last—collaboration.

I would also like to thank Auburn's Kirk Sampson and Shelly Poe, Alabama's Jeff Purinton, Georgia's Claude Felton, LSU's Michael Bonnette, Texas A&M's Alan Cannon and Brad Marquardt, Ohio State's Jerry Emig, Tennessee's Jimmy Stanton and the SEC's Herb Vincent for their help on this project.

My wife, Linda (we have been married twenty-four years), has always been there with love and understanding. I often joke that she has loved me all these years without really knowing what I did for a living. It reminds me of a line said about her years ago by Wimp Sanderson, the former basketball coach at Alabama. Sanderson said: "Of course, Linda is a physician, but when it comes to being married to

Paul, the only thing that can be said is that she has a lot of book sense, but no common sense."

Finally, there is group of people I can't thank more than the callers of our show. I have had many of them tell me either to my face or on the air that the show could not exist without them. And since the list of those who uttered that line is endless, I'll simply say thanks to all of the folks who made the Finebaum audience the best in the business. Obviously, I have met only a fraction of those who call and listen, but . . .

So to Jim from Tuscaloosa, I-Man, Legend, Tammy, Darriel, K-Dub, Charles from Reeltown, Phyllis from Mulga, Robert from Iowa, and the tens of thousands of people for whom I've never met—but share the common goal of loving college football, particularly boasting about the SEC—many thanks and my eternal gratitude.

Of the many stories I have heard over the years in relation to the show, perhaps, one of my favorites comes courtesy of my wife.

She knew a middle-aged woman who one day thanked her for our show. Perplexed, my wife asked why the compliment.

"Well, after my mother died, I ended up having to spend a lot of time with my father, and quite frankly, we had never gotten along and had absolutely nothing in common," said the woman to Linda. "Being in a big family, he was much closer to my brothers. But one day, I was visiting him and your husband's show was on and he was riveted to everything that was being said. He listened every day for four hours. He built his day around the program. So I started listening and suddenly, for the first time in our lives, we had something in common. When we were together, that's what we talked about and after nearly a lifetime of having a strained relationship, it brought us closer together and we finally had something to talk about."

I was honored to help.

About the Authors

Paul Finebaum is a college football analyst for ESPN and host of a daily national radio show heard on ESPN and SiriusXM and simulcast on the SEC Network. He has also been a regular contributor to ESPN's College *GameDay*, as well as *SportsCenter*. He previously was an award-winning investigative reporter and newspaper columnist in Alabama, and several collections of his columns have been published. He has appeared on numerous television programs, including *60 Minutes*, *Nancy Grace* and *Morning Joe*. He has been honored by numerous universities, from Columbia University to his alma mater, the University of Tennessee. Finebaum lives in Charlotte.

Gene Wojciechowski is a columnist for ESPN.com and a regular contributor to ESPN's College *GameDay*, as well as ESPN's golf majors telecasts. Before joining ESPN in 1998, he worked as a sports reporter for the *Chicago Tribune*, the *Los Angeles Times*, and other publications. His work has been honored by the Football Writers Association of America, the Associated Press Sports Editors, and has been featured in the annual Best American Sports Writing series. He has authored or coauthored nine other books, including the bestseller *The Last Great Game: Duke Vs. Kentucky*. Wojciechowski lives in Wheaton, Illinois.